Praise for *From Sabotage to Support*

"Packed with everyday wisdom and common-sense recommendations, *From Sabotage to Support* provides an important alternative to our oppositional, combative social milieu. The authors offer insights, analyses, strategies, and everyday wisdom that give us the necessary tools to transform our workplaces into more equitable, harmonious, inclusive spaces."
—**AnaLouise Keating, PhD, Professor and Doctoral Program Director, Department of Multicultural Women's and Gender Studies, Texas Woman's University, and Gloria Anzaldúa scholar**

"*From Sabotage to Support* is a fantastic addition to the body of knowledge for women (and allies) by women. This book lays down a solid foundation for people new to feminist and womanist journeys while providing immensely actionable guidance for managing our sabotaging behaviors toward ourselves and others. The authors thoughtfully include myriad diverse identities and movements that define the complex human experience. This book will forever change you, your workplace, and the way that you embrace and connect with people."
—**Tiffany Jana, DM, CEO, TMI Portfolio, and coauthor of *Overcoming Bias* and *Erasing Institutional Bias***

"Wiggins and Anderson have written a profound book to help us understand the role of patriarchal systems and how we can move from sabotage to support. This is a must-read for white women and women of color who are interested in how we can reclaim our voice and power and develop collaborative, authentic relationships across racial lines and create a new reality of support."
—**Judith H. Katz, EdD, author of *White Awareness*, coauthor of *Safe Enough to Soar*, and Executive Vice President, The Kaleel Jamison Consulting Group, Inc.**

"The timeliness of *From Sabotage to Support* can't be overstated. As an employer of a diverse group of individuals, thanks to the teachings in this book, I am now acutely aware of how I have helped perpetuate the patriarchy by rewarding workplace behaviors that originated with a system designed by white men to benefit only them. This book opens up a space for women to discuss how we're unwittingly supporting the continuation of this system. As Wiggins and Anderson

show us, we've been working against one another. By working together as a group, as seen in the Women's Marches and the #MeToo
movement and outlined in this book, we have a greater opportunity
to better women's lives when we lift each other up. The workplace
can be competitive, but it doesn't have to be. This enlightening book
provides us with new tools to help white women recognize our privilege and our bias and change the way we lead as employers and the
way we work as employees."

—Liz Bradford, owner of Bradford Public Relations Inc.

From Sabotage to Support

From *SABOTAGE* *to* SUPPORT

A New Vision for Feminist Solidarity
in the Workplace

Joy L. Wiggins and
Kami J. Anderson

BK

Berrett–Koehler Publishers, Inc.

MAY '19

491 5000

Berrett-Koehler Publishers, Inc.
1333 Broadway, Suite 1000
Oakland, CA 94612-1921

Tel: (510) 817-2277   Fax: (510) 817-2278   www.bkconnection.com

ORDERING INFORMATION

QUANTITY SALES. Special discounts are available on quantity purchases by corporations, associations, and others. For details, contact the "Special Sales Department" at the Berrett-Koehler address above.

INDIVIDUAL SALES. Berrett-Koehler publications are available through most bookstores. They can also be ordered directly from Berrett-Koehler: Tel: (800) 929-2929; Fax: (802) 864-7626; www.bkconnection.com.

ORDERS FOR COLLEGE TEXTBOOK / COURSE ADOPTION USE. Please contact Berrett-Koehler: Tel: (800) 929-2929; Fax: (802) 864-7626.

Distributed to the U.S. trade and internationally by Penguin Random House Publisher Services.

Berrett-Koehler and the BK logo are registered trademarks of Berrett-Koehler Publishers, Inc.

Printed in United States of America

Berrett-Koehler books are printed on long-lasting acid-free paper. When it is available, we choose paper that has been manufactured by environmentally responsible processes. These may include using trees grown in sustainable forests, incorporating recycled paper, minimizing chlorine in bleaching, or recycling the energy produced at the paper mill.

Library of Congress Cataloging-in-Publication Data

Names: Wiggins, Joy L., author. | Anderson, Kami J., author.
Title: From sabotage to support : a new vision for feminist solidarity in the workplace / Joy L. Wiggins, Kami J. Anderson.
Description: 1st Edition. | Oakland, CA : Berrett-Koehler Publishers, 2019.
Identifiers: LCCN 2018053314 | ISBN 9781523098477 (paperback)
Subjects: LCSH: Women—Employment. | Feminism. | Solidarity. | BISAC: BUSINESS & ECONOMICS / Workplace Culture. | SOCIAL SCIENCE / Feminism & Feminist Theory.
Classification: LCC HD6053 .W464 2019 | DDC 650.1/3082—dc23
LC record available at https://lccn.loc.gov/2018053314

First Edition

25 24 23 22 21 20 19   10 9 8 7 6 5 4 3 2 1

Cover design: Alvaro Villanueva / Bookish Design. Cover art: Delmaine Donson/ iStock. Book interior production and design: VJB/Scribe. Copyedit: Lunaea Weatherstone. Proofreader: Nancy Bell. Index: Sylvia Coates.

I dedicate this book to my mother, Cynthia, and my sisters, Amy and Liz, who have been the ultimate models of woman power, and to my daughter, Ruby, who embraces the next generation of women leaders wholeheartedly.

—Joy

I dedicate this book to my tribe of sisters, of blood and love, but most of all to my daughter, goddaughters, nieces, and loves who look to us as women for models of support, strength, and solidarity.

—Kami

CONTENTS

Contents

Contents

The Path to Liberation

> To show up as my authentic self at work, I need to be supported and seen as a woman of color (WOC) with talent, skills, and experiences that add value and worth to the work and organizational culture. I need to have allies truly listen and learn from our stories, and support WOC in our leadership and ask us, "How can we support you?" I would feel seen and validated and asked about my experiences from my multiplicity of identities and allowed space and grace to flex my leadership. This sometimes means de-centering whiteness from the room or conversation, and having white folks take a back seat and allow people of color to process and figure out what is best for them at that time.
>
> — Michele, Filipinx-American,
> 43, immigration attorney

What does it mean to be authentic? The dictionary says something that's authentic is "representing one's true nature or beliefs; true to oneself or to the person identified." When we started writing this book, we asked several women, "If you could present your authentic self in the workplace, what would that look like?" Dictionary aside, defining the word "authentic" can be tricky because authenticity looks different to everyone. Being authentic in the workplace — and everywhere else — can be liberating and invigorating. We believe it is possible to achieve authenticity, but it's going to take all of us to get there. It will take time and involve sincere, ongoing efforts. There will be some discomfort along the way and difficult but rewarding conversations; there will be times when we may have varying opinions on what equality and true liberation should look like. Liberation for women may be attaining equal access and representation in all spheres of influence politically, economically, and socially. Liberation is the ability to bring that authentic self to all aspects of our lives. Identifying as women might be where our similarities end, and this might make it challenging to build a relationship. But it is possible.

Before we solve the problem, we have to define it. What is keeping women from being present and authentic? We call it out as sabotage. We define sabotage as the unconscious or conscious undermining of another woman in a competitive, predominantly patriarchal, and/or white supremacist structure. This can take many forms, but it mostly comes down to using one's power position to damage or weaken another woman's access to an opportunity, promotion, or voice being heard equitably. Our firm belief is that in order to see these changes through, we need to talk about sabotage. We need to name it and address it, because if we don't, true liberation and authenticity and bringing our authentic selves to work will continue to be intangible. To be clear, our definition of sabotage dismantles the notion that women are somehow genetically meant to be backstabbers and cruel to each other — this is an outdated and patently incorrect notion that was, and continues to be, commonly used to pit women against each other. What's really at play is that we, as women, are still forced to exist in a system that gives some people power and privilege, and gives others nothing. It is manipulation of this power and privilege that results in sabotage over support.

We have interviewed more than seventy-five women from different age groups, geographic regions, occupations, races, ethnicities, sexual orientations, and abilities on the topic of authenticity and sabotage. The stories they shared indicate a collective understanding of these women's experiences and backgrounds. We have sprinkled some of these stories and examples throughout the book. You might empathize and easily connect with these women's experiences, but others may be completely foreign to you. Those are perhaps the most important ones. All experiences are valid, and all are worth hearing.

There are plenty of cases that give evidence to the fact that women are supporting each other. According to studies by Catalyst, *Harvard Business Review*, and *Forbes*, despite the pitfalls of the workforce in terms of the wage gap, gender bias, and the motherhood penalty, women support each other even more so than men.[1] And that's great — but there are also many times when women sabotage and undermine each other, and that's what we aim to correct.

Who We Are

The way our experiences have shaped us and how we continue to shape our experiences informs the way we interpret the world. For instance, Joy identifies as a white, queer woman, and her experience growing up white and a woman informs the way she moves through the world in a very particular way. The world shapes her and she in turn shapes the world. Kami identifies as an African American woman, but her experiences are shaped by being born after the civil rights movement and being raised at the height of the women's independence movement. This position has influenced not only how she sees the world but how she sometimes demands the world sees her. But she's clear these demands don't always work in her favor. Both of us are diversity and inclusion coaches who hold regular workshops and speaking events to help women in the workplace recognize implicit bias and power dynamics and how these two things impact daily interactions, relationships, and other experiences both professionally and personally.

What to Expect

In chapter 1, we discuss the history of and the sidelined voices of women of color by taking a look at the women's liberation movement. While white American women were fighting for the right to vote, and equal rights across the board, what was going on in communities of color? The purpose of this chapter is to examine how power dynamics can pit us against each other. This also illuminates how those of us with privilege can use it to benefit women without privilege, which we'll discuss throughout the book.

In chapters 2, 3, and 4 we really break down these socialized behaviors that trigger implicit bias and microaggressions. We will explore privilege, patriarchy, and other socialized ideologies that choke our supportive efforts. By becoming aware of how we behave through this socialization, we are beginning to identify the weeds of negative thoughts and patterns that could undermine our garden of support. In chapter 5, you will be given tools to pull out those weeds at the root so we can nurture our support without distraction. These final chapters show us how we can engage our authentic selves, and a sense of allyship and a sense of liberation, when we finally take off our masks and show up as women for women.

We also introduce some terms that we use in the book that might be new to you or perhaps need some clarification. These include: feminism, patriarchy, bias, microaggressions, hierarchy, intersectionality, and womanism. You can find these definitions in Appendix A at the end of the book.

We absolutely do not expect you to close this book and instantly arrive at the destination of support. But we do expect you, and those you coach, to engage in self-reflection. We expect questions to arise. We expect conversations to begin. We want to be clear that this work will not be completed within a year — it may even take longer. But we need to get started. Many of us have been doing this work in isolation, in private and seclusion, and it is time for us to join those who have been working on the front lines.

Why This Book? Why Now?

This book stems from research Joy did in 2007, while working at her previous institution in Texas. She would later revive the research at a women's professional networking talk on how women could better support each other. After the talk, the women in the room had lots of comments and stories, and Joy knew she might need to resurface this study. She went on to do a TEDx talk at Western Washington University titled "From Sabotage to Support: Women Liberating Women in the Workplace." As she started talking about this work again, all kinds of women continued to enthusiastically nod their heads and say, "Oh, have I got a story for you!" Joy has followed up and recorded many of those stories that showcase how this insidious and often subtle form of intragroup oppression happens in ways that we might not be aware of. Many women have asked her what we can do to decrease the wage gap, have better experiences at work, stop sabotaging, and improve women's lives in general.

Joy and Kami started talking about women's experiences specifically in academia when we met in Spain at a seminar on intercultural communication in 2015. We both felt the seminar didn't dig deeply enough into what communication looks like across different social identities. As we started to collaborate on a variety of projects, we wanted to find a way to bring women together across our many differences. Kami introduced Joy to womanism, originally introduced by Alice Walker, which amplified the voice of black women and uncovered how feminism in general did not fully address the concerns of black women. As we continued discussing issues in academia around women, we found that perhaps the real issue is between white women and women of color. Now, with the surge of feminism resurfacing in new ways, this is the time, *our* time to come together across differences to transform, liberate, and bear witness to the changing tide where all women come together in solidarity.

The Beginnings

Both of us are professors and academics who work and have worked in academia, and have done much research around cultural identity, intercultural communication, critical race theory, and privilege. Joy has done research on this particular topic since 2007, when she experienced it firsthand at a Texas university. Her first year as a professor, she found one woman in particular would not only undermine her ideas, she would also comment on Joy's body and say how fat she used to be but then must have lost a lot of weight. Once this colleague caught Joy in an elevator and said, "Oh, my gosh, you have lost so much weight, I can't believe how big you were before. I mean, you were huge!" and as she said this, she used her hands to show how large Joy's breasts had been. As Joy left the elevator, clearly aghast at this fat-shaming and backhanded compliment, she saw that the

woman seemed shocked at her own behavior, as if she realized what she had just said. Joy went back to her office and
wondered if this happened to other women, if they too got
caught up in "mean girl" syndrome. This type of behavior
reminded her of those middle-school "catfights" where girls
compete for the attention of the boys. The boys were now
the men in power at her institution and the women who
colluded with them. This behavior goes beyond the workplace, and the term "catfight" is used to make it seem sexy
that women are fighting to the amusement of men on the
sidelines. Sabotage isn't always evidenced by overt, explicit
behaviors; it can also be subtle and covert, making the
other person feel confused, unsettled, and demeaned. These
types of microaggressions may not have ill intent, but the
impact on the other person is still damaging.[2] It turns out,
Joy's time at this institution ultimately proved to be a toxic
work environment, with women behaving in inappropriate ways toward each other, with men on the periphery. Joy
has heard many similar stories since then. Kami has one
of them.

Kami had historically overlooked the ways in which we
sabotage or hurt one another as women within our own
groups. She leaned on the obvious examples she was able
to identify between women of color and white women,
and most times she marginalized or flat-out ignored the
instances among women of color. She naively attributed
this behavior as a response to mistreatment from whites, or
the need to feel worthy in those spaces, but never thought
that it was also linked to a patriarchal system. Not only was
Kami blind to the true connection between the two, she saw
it from the position of a perpetrator. In one instance, she
distanced herself from colleagues she believed fit too much
into the "angry black woman" stereotype. In a moment
of self-reflection that came from an outright rejection of
friendship with a colleague, Kami realized that she too can
be part of the problem — and she was.

It was this piece of her "baggage" that connected Kami and Joy in Spain. The candid conversations they had about how the women in the group engaged with one another, the facilitator (also a woman), and the few men present during that weeklong intensive sparked reflective conversations about women, interactions, and liberation. Kami did not bat an eye when Joy called her about writing a book. She was clear they both had something to say that could enhance how we show up for one another.

Smash the Patriarchy!

Male-dominated workplaces and social norms create a system in which women don't have equal voice, power, or representation, thus making it unfair, unjust, and disempowering. A patriarchal system is where men have authority and power over women in all aspects of society — politically, economically, and culturally. In the United States in particular, the hierarchy puts white men at the top. This unequal and competitive system creates a breeding ground for women to undercut each other in ways they may not even be aware of. Behaviors such as backbiting, gossiping, taking credit for work that isn't ours, and making passive-aggressive comments that undermine one's sense of belonging and worth are all part of this competitive culture. These are some of the more flagrant behaviors that are easy to identify. There are also subtle behaviors such as dismissing the experiences of other women because they may not have been your experience or falling silent when you see another woman falling victim to microaggressions. The extreme examples are easy for us to separate ourselves from because we are very clear about whether or not these behaviors are present in our workplace. But the more subtle behaviors that rely on the power of silence or silencing require more self-reflection and digging deeper into our space within the patriarchal system.

Women tend to sabotage each other if their environment is dominated by competition, top-down leadership, and lack of collaboration and trust. A small but relevant diversion here: In Australia, there's a saying "cut down the tall poppies," meaning to cut down those who stand out. In a journal article, this phrase was used to refer to women working in academia who cut each other down when they are successful. If women are working under a system that they didn't create or have much voice in, they will adopt the top-down, gritty competitive culture and like Shelley Taylor has said, invoke the fight-or-flight mode as reactions to their stress.[3] She contends that women should adopt the "tend-and-befriend" method, where they might turn to friends and family. But what about colleagues at work?

Sabotage can also take the form of the "queen bee syndrome," coupled with ageism. We have heard many stories in which women claim that a senior and older woman aligned herself with the men in power and saw the sexist practices as a rite of passage to endure to gain access to leadership positions — the idea being that it's best not to rock the boat when addressing sexist behavior. The reverse has also been true, where younger women negate the contributions of the older women in the office because they are "outdated." Jessica Bennett claims that 95 percent of women have felt undercut by another woman.[4] Sabotage can take the form of minimizing a woman's contribution based along lines of race, sexual orientation, gender identity, class, educational level, ethnicity, age, ability, size, and so on. This might also be in the form of the maternal wall, where women discuss whether to have children, whether or when they should return to work after having children, breast versus bottle feeding, among many other ways we judge and compare ourselves. These personal comparisons inevitably seep into the workplace.

In her 2002 book *Catfight: Rivalries among Women, from Diets to Dating, from the Boardroom to the Delivery Room*, Leora Tanenbaum discusses how women are socialized to compete with respect to beauty, motherhood, class and racial lines, and dating. She discusses how women are caught up in covert competition and perpetual vertigo of striking a balance between the old, traditional rules and the new: by working to pay the bills but not neglecting our children, by working out and staying healthy but not too much to incite jealousy in our friends, and "by getting married but having an egalitarian relationship" and "wearing lipstick and mascara but unapologetically eating lasagna and ice cream." The vertigo situation hasn't changed, but perhaps the context has from 2002 when she wrote *Catfight* to our current reality under Trump, #MeToo, and the immigration crisis in 2018.

THE PROCESS

For women to move from sabotage to support, we must engage in a cyclical process that moves from looking at the self, then outward to society and other women, and then back to the self. This is a continued journey of self-examination to examining our society and environment. Women can begin to undo or dismantle these systems by first understanding our feminist cultural history and the key players across racial, class, sexuality, and geographic boundaries. In this book, we push back on the generalized usage of the term "intersectionality" and explore how it has once again sidelined black women's voices in particular. There are many different feminist movements that illustrate the rich tapestry of diverse struggles toward liberation. When all of these movements are taught and incorporated into our collective knowledge of history, solidarity and liberation are more easily attainable. Movements like womanism, black feminism, mujerista, and indigenous (Native and First Nations) are all seeking ways to transform these male dominated systems. As women, it is our duty to learn our history to better inform the ways we can come together in solidarity across our differences. If we don't know our history, our current reality can never be changed.

The second way we can start to "smash the patriarchy" is to take a good look at the stories we tell ourselves. We can start with how we view who we are as women and the way we talk to ourselves. Typically, the messages that run rampant through our heads that go unmonitored and unchecked — judgments about our sense of worth and belonging in the world — put us in a negative narrative loop of incorrect assumptions, ideas, and opinions we hold about ourselves and others. These messages stem from various forms of media like television, movies, news, magazines, websites, social media, and other forms of digital content. Remember movies like *The First Wives Club, Mean Girls, Stepmom, The Devil Wears Prada,* fairy tales about the younger woman and the older crone or witch, and television shows like *The Real Housewives of* [*Wherever*] among many other television shows where women compete for power or the attention of men. What we tell ourselves manifests itself into the world, so when society tells us that we are only valuable based on our body size or beauty and not our brains, we internalize this. This is a vicious cycle that repeats itself: society tells we aren't worthy, we internalize it, and keep repeating the story to ourselves.

When we rebel, we tend to act out, get angry, and experience a range of emotions from underlying simmering rage to muted anger, to guilt, to shame, to self-sabotage. We might retreat because we start to feel crazy — everyone else seems to be accepting the status quo. We go back into our safe place of complacency. We get angry and then feel guilty about it because we are supposed to keep taking the pill, swallow it and allow ourselves to accept messages about losing weight, being nice but still being unworthy, and allowing men to dictate the culture that we inhabit. The worst part is that we tend to put each other back into those boxes to make sure we all keep the storyline going. Consider again cutting the tall poppies. *If I can't get ahead, then neither can you.* This crucial step in taking apart or deconstructing our narrative loop is so key in undoing this tangled mess of body image, leadership style, and sabotaging behaviors.

A Day in the Liberated Life!

If all the women who read this book did the things we suggest, here's a perfect world scenario for what everyday life would look like:

- You would show up to life fully actualized and able to state your needs to sustain an appropriate work/life balance.

- Your interests and your full self (everything that makes you you) in all its identities would not only be included but embraced and encouraged.

- You would feel supported in stating your needs and desires. Your projects and ideas would be respected and heard. When you received feedback, it would be respectful and helpful.

- You would be able to collaborate easily and have faith that everyone is working toward the same goal, without tallying every little task being divided up equally but having faith that it's all for the same expected end.

Through our work as academics and entrepreneurs, we have seen that the more women know about their history, their social conditioning, their varying degrees of power and privilege, and their biases, the better equipped they are to stand in solidarity with each other. This book addresses how women have stood in each other's way or sabotaged each other throughout history. We contend that if we learn from our differing histories, our biases, and our own internalized oppression and come together across those differences, we can push equity forward for all of us, rather than just for some of us. The ability to identify and curb sabotage makes it possible for us to push past it. Knowing what sabotage is breaks open those locked doors of miscommunication and isolation so that we can move toward empowerment, solidarity, and, finally, liberation to be our authentic selves in whatever way that looks like for us.

As women — and individuals — we have power in some places and not others. This book is built on the notion that our varying identities, which run the gamut from age to ability and everything in between, and many other factors, contribute to how we think and behave. It is necessary to examine how power and privilege play out in these experiences; otherwise, it will be harder for us to understand how to connect with other women.

Moving Forward

The primary purpose of this book is to teach you how you can offer this sense of inclusion, and end to sabotage, to any person, organization, group, or class you may work with. We have included a range of women's voices to explore how sabotage happens and what we can do to stop it. We can only do this if we come together, all of us, across difference, in solidarity and commitment to the transformation *of* and liberation *from* patriarchy.

Secondly, we want to better understand how our own internalized oppression has prevented these efforts to move forward from happening. The lack of articulation around the insidious nature of women sabotaging each other and how we can better support each other in hostile workplaces goes unnoticed because we don't want to talk about that dirty elephant in the room. We also don't want the idea of backbiting and sabotaging behavior to be used as fodder for antifeminism rhetoric or perpetuating misogynistic behavior. For instance, a male nurse told us, "Yeah, I know all the nurses in my area are constantly backbiting each other and fighting. I just try to stay out of it," and "I've noticed that too and can't understand why women are so mean to each other." Many times, when we don't realize these workplaces are hostile and toxic, we abide by the rules and norms set forth just to survive. Hostility and toxicity might look different across occupations, geographic regions, generations, and types of institutions in which we work. On the surface it may appear as if these negative elements are part of every workplace, but if you look closely, and if the workplace doesn't have a good number of diverse employees, leaders, and equitable policies, then you might find more hostile and toxic experiences.

We believe this book is applicable to everyone because it speaks to the hidden biases that we all have and the power those biases and privileges have to uphold patriarchal systems, thus stifling the magic that happens when everyone has equitable chances at what they want for their lives. But this book is only the beginning. We need to make it clear that you can't truly achieve liberation unless you start to embody the journey. It's not a packaged toolkit or single workshop complete with actionable items that you can check off a list and success is yours. This is a lifetime of deconstructing, unpacking, and picking away at generations of socialization passed down over generations. Every day will bring a new awareness and a new challenge, but it is our hope that you will feel empowered and liberated more and more so that you can hold that space for your sisters to also move in transformational directions.

CHAPTER 1

A Brief History of Feminist Movements

To go to work and show up in my own skin ... no code switching. In order for me to show up as my authentic self, white people need first acknowledge and know the impact that American history has on people of color and then help marginalized folks with the privilege that they have. Men also need to acknowledge their privilege and allow women to lead. How would this feel? I imagine it would be liberating. I would have a sense of freedom. Freedom to be my authentic self. Period.

— Tessa, African American Caribbean, 46, professor

Throughout this chapter, we provide a foundation for our feminist cultural history from a different perspective than the one we might have learned in school or college. We will look at how women became divided early in the first wave of the feminist movement and throughout the subsequent second, third, and fourth waves. The term "waves" might connote a monolithic and unified agenda around one set of ideas where in fact it contains a variety of issues around different ideas at different times perpetuated by different women.[1] We examine how that division has kept us from gaining equity with men in substantial and sustainable ways, thus leading to sabotaging behaviors. Let's be clear, we believe sabotage occurred long before feminism's first wave, in extremely violent ways under slavery: women encouraging their husbands to beat female slaves or doing it themselves, forcing other women to work while ill, and turning a blind eye while plantation masters raped black women (think Mistress Epps and her treatment of Patsey in the movie 12 *Years a Slave*).[2] But we will begin with the movements in the 1800s.

First-Wave Feminism from 1800 to 1920

No, this isn't an American History Ph.D. candidate's dissertation. We need to establish background before we get into modern times. So let's begin with a brief history, starting in the 1800s and going to the 1920s, during feminism's important first wave. It helps to start by establishing who was doing what and when. If you recall your high school history class, the Seneca Falls Convention likely rings a bell. After Elizabeth Cady Stanton and Lucretia Mott were barred from the World Anti-Slavery Convention in London in 1840 because women were not allowed to participate, they decided to organize. The Seneca Falls Convention in New York was held in July 1848, with 300 people in attendance, mostly women. Together, they debated and signed the Declaration of Sentiments, which its author Stanton modeled after the Declaration of Independence.

However, many of us may not know that, long before Seneca Falls, women activists of color were already working in their communities to not only abolish slavery but to also obtain the right to vote. Maria W. Stewart, a black teacher and journalist who was born of free parents but placed in servitude after their untimely death when she was five, was the first American woman to give a speech to a mixed gender audience. Between 1831 and 1832, she gave four speeches in Boston to organizations like the African-American Female Intelligence Society specifically about the plight of African American women.[3] At the prompting of editor William Lloyd Garrison, she started writing for his abolitionist magazine *The Liberator*. Stewart was also the first black woman to lecture about women's rights and make a public antislavery speech, in addition to Ida B. Wells and Sojourner Truth.[4]

The white women's movement started gaining momentum before the start of the Civil War (1861–1865). We separate the two movements because white women created a rift along racial lines. They allowed Southern antiabolitionist women and other political factions to influence them, convincing them that the only way to get the vote was to sideline black men and women in order to appease a racist majority.[5] The dialogue became that of the supposed inferiority of black people, and maintaining the presumed superior white race became a major part of their actions.

Passed in 1850, the Fugitive Slave Act allowed slave owners from the South to recapture escaped slaves. The Civil War had not yet started, so it was even more urgent for black people to be freed and get the vote. They were facing escalated violence, as angry white Southerners began to lose their free (slave) labor. In that same year, the first National Women's Rights Convention commenced. Stakes were higher for the collaboration between the women's movement and the abolitionist movement. It was at these conventions that Frederick Douglass, Susan B. Anthony, Lucy Stone, Elizabeth Cady Stanton, and Sojourner Truth all came together. At this time, William Lloyd Garrison and other men of the Republican Party were also speaking up for women's rights and abolition.

In 1851, Sojourner Truth gave her famous speech "Ain't I a Woman?" at the Ohio Women's Rights Convention, while she was working tirelessly on both the abolitionist and women's movements. Other women such as Ida B. Wells, Josephine St. Pierre Ruffin, and Mary Church Terrell were all speaking, writing, and organizing for both women's rights and abolition. The split occurred around 1866 after the Civil Rights Act passed, granting former slaves and women equal protection under the law but not the vote. In 1870, the Fifteenth Amendment gave voting rights to all men with equal protection under the law — but not women. The ratification of this amendment caused Susan B. Anthony and Frederick Douglass to go their separate ways. Douglass was worried about the growing violence that former slaves and black people were facing from Southern backlash following the Civil War. Anthony *and* Stanton both asserted, on numerous occasions, that they would rather see white people gain the vote over former slaves and black people.

. . . .

A Difference in Ideology

At Steinway Hall, a concert hall in New York, in 1869, Stanton said, "Shall American statesmen ... so amend their constitutions as to make their wives and mothers the political inferiors of unlettered and unwashed ditch-diggers, bootblacks, butchers and barbers, fresh from the slave plantations of the South?" To this, Douglass replied, "When women, because they are women, are hunted down through the cities of New York and New Orleans; when they are dragged from their houses and hung from lampposts; when their children are torn from their arms and their brains dashed out upon the pavement; when they are objects of insult and rage at every turn; when they are in danger of having their homes burnt down ... then they will have an urgency to obtain the ballot equal to our own."[6] This exchange prompted the division between the women's suffrage and abolitionist movements.

....

PROMINENT BLACK WOMEN IN THE MOVEMENT IN THE 1800S

Simultaneously during this time, black women were pushing for female and racial equity. Josephine St. Pierre Ruffin, a prominent black speaker and suffragette, started the American Woman Suffrage Association in 1869 with two white women, Lucy Stone and Julia Ward Howe. Twenty-three years later, in 1892, Harriet Tubman, Ida B. Wells, Frances Harper, and Ruffin started the first National Association for Colored Women. The problem was that cultural perspectives didn't shift even after the Civil War or the Fifteenth Amendment. White women were using women of color as domestic workers, thus furthering their privilege and desire to access cheap labor. By 1890, the census revealed that there were 2.7 million young black women and girls working at domestic jobs that weren't much different from the slave conditions they thought they had escaped. Sexual assault was still prevalent in the white households in which they worked. In addition, black women working in agriculture were made to sign contracts that could be used against them if their employers decided they were owed more hours or money.

The last ten years of the nineteenth century proved to be dangerous for black people — living *and* working in America. Violence was at an all-time high and was becoming normalized through laws of segregation in the South, and persistent limited economic opportunities in the North. At the same time, white women were continually banding together to enable white supremacy to be more fully entrenched in the movement by not allowing women of color into their meetings, and taking on the agenda of Southern white women — whose racism was anything but implicit.

By 1896, the National League of Colored Women and the First National Conference of Colored Women emerged as organizations focusing specifically on women of color. Activist and educator Mary Church Terrell led the National League of Colored Women as the most influential woman in the organization. These organizations focused on strategizing against the inhumane conditions of domestic work, assaults on black women's image, and anti-lynching laws. Simultaneously, white men were pressuring white women to support white interests over those of people of color so the white women could move closer to getting the vote. It was a very clear line in the sand — organizations founded and run by white women continued to ignore the plight of people of color, immigrants, refugees, and poor working-class whites.

THE NINETEENTH AMENDMENT

Let's fast-forward to 1920, when the Nineteenth Amendment was finally passed. Technically, this amendment gave *all* women the right to vote, though for a time it functionally only applied to white women. Black women were disenfranchised in the South, and other women of color were not extended this right through various racist structures that were in place. At this time, potential voters were required to pass literacy tests; this, and additional limitations in access to polls made voting difficult for black women. Every time one barrier was removed, another one came along to replace it. The goalpost kept moving, and the laws kept making it harder for people of color to vote. Native women couldn't vote until 1924, Asian American women were barred until 1952, and black women were given the right to vote as late as 1964, so to say "women" got the right to vote in 1920 is limited, to say the least.

The Second Wave: Civil and Reproductive Rights

Feminism's second wave was much informed by the civil rights movement that took place in 1950s and 1960s. What was called the women's liberation movement would come into fruition and inform politics via such programs as the President's Commission on the Status of Women, chaired by Eleanor Roosevelt and established by President Kennedy in 1961 to advise him on the status of women's issues. Rather than ratifying the Equal Rights Amendment, which would give women equal rights under the law, Kennedy thought the commission could satisfy his labor base, which believed that women needed their own protected legislation for workplace accommodations to avoid workplace injury and exploitation. The protected legislation just reinforced employers to only hire men so they could avoid making any special accommodations for women.[7]

After they were ousted from a political conference because they wanted to talk about women's issues, Jo Freeman and Shulamith Firestone created the newsletter "Voice of the Women's Liberation Movement" in 1967, which popularized the term "women's liberation movement." With the inception of the National Organization for Women (NOW), spearheaded by Betty Friedan (author of *The Feminine Mystique*), second-wave feminism prompted the Equal Rights Amendment, Title IX, and Title VII. Title IX gives women equal access to college sports, and Title VII bans sexual harassment from the workplace. Unfortunately, the Equal Rights Amendment, as of 2018, has still not passed. However, we want to pay close attention to the voices of the women who have continually been marginalized in the feminist movement.

What we find in the second wave are sidelined voices shouting their needs to the players on the field. The players from the first wave were those who benefited primarily from the feminist movement: white women. The voices of those representing racial, ethnic, and sometimes even sexual heritages and opinions were relegated to the bench and the stands as this movement progressed. But before we dig into the second wave, let's take another look at womanism. It was womanism that cleared the path for the other movements of this wave to flourish in ways that, as we will see in the subsequent waves of feminism, changed the understanding of what it means to address equity among women. This liberation of the wholeness of our womanhood is the foundation of the undergraduate pedagogy that has followed Kami especially for most of her adult life.

During this second wave, reproductive health was a major issue that privileged white women's voices over women of color, along with equal pay for equal work, domestic violence, sexual harassment, and maternity leave. Systems like health care, education, politics, and human services, in addition to nonprofits and corporations, are most often set up with a top-down hierarchical structure. Women have not had an equal voice in the construction of these entities. Women of color fare far worse in the issues around reproductive and sexual health. Let's take a look at how the first-wave women informed the second wave's approach to reproductive rights.

In the first wave, a few exceptions set the stage for the reemergence of reproductive rights in the second wave. Sarah

Grimke, writer and Quaker, was mostly active in abolition, but started to garner more speaking engagements on the subject of "voluntary motherhood." In 1850, her book *Marriage* maintained that women ought to have the right to decide when and if they wanted children, and should have the right to refuse sex with their husbands.

She continued that both women and men should be educated about what is called "family planning" today. At the time, it was a revolutionary — and maligned — idea because women were encouraged to have as many children as possible. However, this fundamental right to decide if and when you wanted children also gave women space to participate in the political process and not be burdened with too many children, if they so desired. Although black women may have felt the same way, their priorities were different, and took the form of preserving their own lives and halting violence above other concerns. Shortly after the Thirteenth Amendment and onward, black women were more or less forcibly sterilized. This extends to today in prisons, both juvenile and adult. Forced sterilization happened among 43 percent of black women during the 1960s and 1970s.[8] There is a long history of forced sterilization among Native, Asian American, and Mexican American men and women.[9] The National Asian Pacific American Women's Forum has been informing policies and activism specifically for Asian American women.[10]

In 1916, Margaret Sanger, a birth control activist, writer, and nurse, opened the first birth control clinic in the mostly black-populated Brownsville neighborhood of Brooklyn. She was arrested nine days later. However, even Sanger spoke prominently at eugenics conferences in which she spoke about weeding out the unfit through sterilization. Proponents of her work suggest that her statements were more about the desire to encourage people to have the children they wanted, and to promote high intelligence, cleanliness, and hard work — while disincentivizing those who did not embody these qualities to breed. This makes what could have been a progressive movement an inherently racist one, as well as paternalistic. It's also worth mentioning that reproductive rights were supported by white women who wanted to work and participate in activities outside the home. For many working-class women — of color and otherwise — that was never an option as they had no choice but to work outside the home *and* manage life inside the home. When these reproductive programs were established, family planning was viewed as a "right" for white women to reduce their family size, and a "duty or moral obligation" to the poor, the working class, and women of color. Classism and racism would work themselves into the reproductive rights movement by dividing women along class lines, especially poor working-class whites, women of color, and immigrants. It was assumed that if working women didn't have as many children, they would have ample resources to pull themselves out of poverty. Obviously, it's not that simple.

Throughout her seminal 1981 book *Women, Race and Class*, Angela Davis outlined the first and second waves' history with reproductive rights in great detail. Notably, she maintains that white feminists might have understood why addressing the abuses of sterilization was so important and might have solidified the movement more had they understood the ramifications to black women. This is our primary takeaway: to express why, as the movement progresses, we can't continually repeat the same mistakes through power and privileged ignorance.

Feminism across Cultures

Although the beginnings of womanism started within the civil rights movement and the black feminist movement, its evolution has influenced similar movements within feminism. Alice Walker coined the term "womanist" in a 1979 short story.[11] It has since evolved into a theoretical framework that holds femininity and culture at its core. Womanism is a social theory that fills the gaps within feminism, and provides a sounding board for the history and experiences of those women who have felt marginalized or excluded from the feminist movement. Some may argue that feminism only acknowledges the feminine aspects of a woman, not the cultural experiences of this same woman. This leaves little to no space for women of color to celebrate both their womanliness and cultural heritage within feminism, and in many ways, they continue to feel that in order to be included, they need to ignore their cultural heritages. During the second wave, these women began to speak out, against the unspoken directive that they choose between their culture and their womanhood. They fought for the inclusion of culture as necessary in order to feel completely part of the feminist movement. To help add some context, let's take a look at some movements it's necessary to be aware of.

Black feminism. Black feminism was born in response to the civil rights movement and the racism within the feminist movement. Historically, black women's role in organizing, campaign canvassing, and marching against Jim Crow segregation was muted and overshadowed by the men who stood at the helm of national leadership and guidance. Noted black feminist scholar Patricia Hill Collins suggested the structures of power designed and maintained by patriarchy also maintain structures of power in regard to race.[12] Therefore, being black and female indicated a double bind of rigid limitations that white women would never experience and refused to acknowledge within the feminist movement.

Chicana feminism/mujerista movement. Chicana feminism emerged to address the ways in which Mexican American women face not only gender bias but also ethnicity, race, and class bias within both the wider Chicano movement and the feminist movement. The Chicana feminist sets her position and existence within and between the male-dominated Chicano movement and the white-centered feminist movement. The mujerista movement looks at the Latinx community as a whole, including the struggles of women within a host of hyphenated ethnicities from the entire region of Latin America, and explores how Latina women can free themselves from the oppressive structures that exist in the region.

Native feminism. Native feminism focuses its activism around tribal sovereignty in addition to gender equity. One of the more popular movements involves the Women of All Red Nations (WARN), established by Madonna Thunderhawk, Lorelei DeCora Means, Phyllis Young, and Janet McCloud in 1974.[13] Their organization was founded in response to incidents like Wounded Knee, uranium mining, and forced sterilization of Native women.[14] Tribal sovereignty can be defined as the right to lead and govern according to traditional values; Native feminist perspectives can bring that distinction to the mutual relationship between land, family, spirit, gender, and self-governance.

White feminism. The distinction of black feminism has given birth to the term "white feminist." It is used as a critique of feminists who do not acknowledge issues of racial and ethnic differences, women who fail to acknowledge intersectionality. A typical argument from white feminists maintains that focusing on race weakens the strength of the movement. If you'll recall, this argument has been the response to many historic moments when the calls from the sidelines became too loud. This perspective — that race somehow muddies the feminist movement — can be understood as a form of sabotage. White feminism has its own forms of racist practices against women of color, as noted in several examples earlier in this chapter. We must understand that conversations about race enrich and add depth to the discussion of feminism and womanhood.

Asian American feminism. It's important not to lump Asian women into one monolithic Asian American experience, because they have vastly different experiences. It's crucial to understand that different experiences require different resources, support, and activism. Right after World War II, as more women of Asian descent were able to immigrate to the United States, there was also an increase in activism by working with battered women's shelters, advocating for refugee and immigration rights, drug prevention programs in Los Angeles, and working against U.S. imperialism.[15] Fighting against stereotypes in the workplace such as dragon lady, or being perceived as weak and exotic (#NotYourAsian-Sidekick),[16] Asian American feminists are combating both racism and sexism.[17]

Arab American feminism. Arab American women have long been involved in activism not only in the United States but globally through helping women in social services and political movements. Examples include Jordanian mothers being able to pass along Jordanian citizenship or combating stereotypes of Arab or Muslim women as meek followers of their husbands.[18] Many women in the movement are advocating for immigration issues, ethnic and religious freedom, working against racial profiling, and protection from police surveillance.[19]

Transfeminism. Transfeminism is a movement by and for trans women who see their liberation bound to the liberation of all women.[20] They maintain that our collective liberation is coming together in solidarity and that everyone should have the right to whatever gender expression they want.

Actively discussing the racial and ethnic differences of women, giving them the opportunity and support to voice their experiences, is one of the solutions to sabotage. These voices can help bring women of color and their issues to the playing field. Once those issues are in the game, advocacy for women of color becomes a larger benefit to the movement.

....

The Third Wave: Power Feminism and the Beauty Myth

Feminism's third wave, which we can date from the 1990s to perhaps the early 2000s (although this is debated), saw women examining sexual harassment, rape culture, and body image. There are those who suggest we are still in the third wave and that this wave is indeed intersectional (more about this in the next section), but we would argue that because this wave lacked the power of technology and social media, it stands on its own.

There's a specific movie that, even though came out in 1980, we feel helped usher in feminism's third wave. *9 to 5* threw a radical, empowering curveball. Dolly Parton, Jane Fonda, and Lily Tomlin starred as three working white women who kidnap their misogynistic boss. In this same year, the Equal Employment Opportunity Commission issued guidelines under Title VII on prohibiting sexual harassment in the office. Anita Hill brought this to a head during the Clarence Thomas hearings eleven years later, in 1991.

The third wave's focus on rape culture and sexual harassment took precedence in legal arenas, but the social arena focused on body image and women in the workplace. Popular culture and art started to change the narrative of the capabilities of women. There were more cultural references to women moving in power positions at work. Television showed powerful women as portrayed in *Buffy the Vampire Slayer*, *The X-Files*, and *Sabrina the Teenage Witch*. Musicians like Missy Elliott, TLC, Destiny's Child, and the Spice Girls were all "bossing it up." However, these powerhouses were also being portrayed as lonely, unfulfilled, and slightly neurotic. Think Diane Keaton leaving her high-powered job to take care of a baby in a farmhouse in *Baby Boom* — she ended up creating her own line of baby food and rocking it — or Demi Moore sexually harassing her colleague Michael Douglas in *Disclosure*, basically doing what men do all the time (but she got caught), and the queen bee syndrome that shows up where these women made it to the top while playing a man's game. They expect other women behind them to do the same. The queen bee syndrome especially is a clear case of sabotage.

Naomi Wolf wrote and spoke out against rape culture on college campuses, and Rebecca Walker wrote "Becoming the Third Wave" in *Ms.* magazine. Walker began her article by saying she couldn't bear to watch the Anita Hill hearings — it was too reminiscent of the O. J. Simpson trial, too much about what Toni Morrison calls the "white gaze," that constant, watchful eye white people level on people of color, and the blaming of black people for things that white people get away with all the time.

In her fierce call to action, Walker clarified the power of the third wave by asking for solidarity among women across differences. She declared that the unrelenting massive attacks on our bodies, our silence, our complicity, our acquiescence for what is baked into our socialization to accept from men, could not stand any longer.

The Fourth Wave: Intersectionality

The fourth wave is what some may term as intersectional. It includes queer, body, trans, and sex positive agendas and is mostly digitally driven. With the rise of social media such as Twitter, Facebook, and YouTube, women have been able to share their experiences, mobilize movements like #MeToo and #TimesUp, and utilize many other hashtags that bring recognition to rape on college campuses and workplace harassment and violence. However, before we continue, we'd like to push back on the term "intersectional." The term comes from examining the law and ethics through a critical race lens. Kimberlé Crenshaw coined this term after examining outright discrimination in police engagement, especially the criminal justice system and the overrepresentation of black women in the prison system.[21] Crenshaw explains, "Because of their intersectional identity as both women and people of color within discourses that are shaped to respond to one or the other, the interests and experiences of women of color are frequently marginalized within both."[22] Even though this concept came from discussions around legal disparities centered on African Americans, Crenshaw's overarching argument is that it is impossible to separate race from gender, class from race, or gender from class when it comes to addressing the needs of an individual. Intersectionality has been used incorrectly inside and outside of feminism. It is important to be clear here: there have been ways in which intersectionality as a term has been universally applied to everyone; however, its actual intent is to directly address racially marginalized groups and the many levels of systemic and cultural discrimination. For example, yes, women are in fact a marginalized group, but Latina women also have to deal with the marginalization that comes from being Latina and woman. African American women have to deal with the discrimination that comes from being woman and black. Native women, Asian women, all face a doubled-down marginalization. The argument for intersectionality is a direct response to the womanist movement, giving us a clearer picture for the *how* we are different and *why* that needs to be acknowledged.

Our understanding of intersectionality as originally presented by Crenshaw is what prompts us to use the term when directly addressing issues involving a convergence of gender, race, and class identities. If all of these three are not present, we prefer to use the term "converging identities." We feel this term maintains the integrity of intersectionality while still acknowledging that we all have multiple identities that can come into play at any given moment in any given situation. Crenshaw's intersectionality challenges us to examine certain narratives from the perspective of race in order to identify the ways we can better support one another.

Learning about some of the women activists of color who are currently mobilizing and doing important work around this issue is essential as we move toward solidarity. For example, Standing Rock activist LaDonna Brave Bull Allard started the Sacred Stone Camp, part of the resistance efforts against the Dakota Access Pipeline.[23] Arab American activists are advocating for LGBTQI+ and immigration rights. For instance, Sandra Khalifa, an Egyptian American, is fighting to uphold the

DREAM Act. Minnesota House Representative Ilhan Omar is the first Somali American elected to U.S. office. She advocates for the civil rights of women from Eastern Africa, seeks to alleviate poverty, and wants to provide free college tuition for families that earn under $125,000 a year.[24] These women are doing amazing work across economic, political, and social issues.

Both Kami and Joy have stories about what it means to exist as a woman in a patriarchal society. We have women in our circles that can cosign or agree to all our stories, but when Kami begins to talk about the ways in which her black female body has been inappropriately sexualized by both men and women without recourse because all black women are sexual objects before they are humans, Joy cannot understand that experience. When Joy talks about the ways in which she may have had to mute her queerness in order to advance, Kami cannot relate. Intersectionality brings the sum total of all the ways in which women can potentially be oppressed in this society and places them on the table, leaving nothing behind.

When it comes to sabotage, one of the biggest taboos is negating intersectionality as unimportant, or claiming intersectionality as "everybody's issue." Both are incorrect. The eye rolls in the conference room when the black woman talks about her struggles with finding a mentor who will boost her professional career, or the term "spicy" used to describe the voiced reactions of the Latina coworker, followed by collective chuckles and giggles from the rest of the office, express why intersectionality is of the utmost. These forms of sabotage communicate to women of color that there is no safe space to talk about how their race and ethnicity also impact their womanhood.

· ·

AUTHOR EXCHANGE
What Is Your Earliest Memory of Feminism?

These sections provide us a space as authors to express our own thoughts and experiences around a topic. In keeping with this chapter, we'll explore our experiences with feminism. There is a concept known as "mirrors and windows," in which a metaphorical mirror allows readers to see themselves in the character or person they are reading about and a window gives them a new perspective, one that they might not have thought of before without having read the character's story.[25] How might you see both mirrors and windows in our experiences? How might these stories help you frame your discussions around your experiences and those of others when discussing your own understanding of feminism?

Joy

Growing up, I was blessed to have strong women in my life. My grandmother and mother were forces to be reckoned with. My grandmother showed me how to protect myself, putting her keys in between each of her fingers and jabbing at potential predators in the mall parking lot. She divorced my grandfather and worked for the army in government contracts for Bell Helicopter for thirty years. She didn't marry her boyfriend of twenty years, refusing to share her money with a man again. My mom was always talking about how women can do anything and instilled in my sisters and me that we had to take care of our money and not let men do it for us.

The first time I started to think about feminism in the workplace was when I was in high school. At my first job in an ice cream shop, my manager harassed me — making comments about my going out with him instead of whatever other guy I was seeing at the time. He was 21. I was 15. I became increasingly mad, but didn't want to rock the boat, so I stayed silent. I knew he had power over me both professionally and physically. By 15, I knew not to trust most men. In fact, I feared them immensely. Eventually, this man made a pass at me. When I told the shop owners, he told them I was lying, and I was fired. This was my first time understanding the power dynamics of sexual harassment. Unfortunately, this was only the beginning for me, and like most women, I didn't always know or understand that it was sexual harassment. I felt that I didn't have a right to complain. I wouldn't really dive into feminism until much later in life — and even now my journey is ongoing.

Kami

My first experiences with feminism came from watching the women around me. Feminism was watching my children's theater director fight to get venues for our plays and being charged by the half hour instead of the hour — but pressing on anyway. Feminism was watching the artistic director of the dance company where I performed fight for space in the male-dominated, highly patriarchal establishment that was West African dance in the United States in the 1970s and 1980s. But these instances were never called feminism.

My first true encounter with feminism was not a positive one. It caused me to do all the things I teach my students not to: I generalized, I stereotyped, I othered. I distanced myself so far away from any association with feminism because I was not going to be *anything* like the woman I met who spent an entire evening bad-mouthing every man in the room, slut-shaming, and marginalizing women who did not share her views or didn't look like her.

I spent much of my childhood on a college campus, and there I encountered a graduate student who was behaving in a rude and obnoxious way to her male counterparts; in hindsight, she may very well have been publicly working out her feminist identity. But it burned me. It burned me because I was young, impressionable, and, quite frankly, could hold a grudge to infinity.

Taking these two things into account, I spent years denying the beast I knew as "feminism" from entering the sanctified gates of my identity. I would hear the word and cringe.

Eventually, I was attracted to womanism because womanists support equity for their racial/ethnic communities just as much as they do their communities of women. Sometimes, we may even sacrifice the women's communities for the greater good of our racial/ethnic communities. Womanists will challenge a feminist who marginalizes a black man and turn around and challenge the same black man if he perpetuates macho tendencies.

· · · · · · · · · · · · · · · · · · · ·

Action Steps

As you read through this book, you will find moments that encourage you to recall your own memories, moments where you will have questions, and moments where you will want to dig a little deeper. In an effort to keep this an intimate exchange between you as the reader and us as the authors, we will provide action steps to help you reflect a bit more, and start to implement strategies in the workplace. These action steps may come from a particular concept in a chapter, from an example or an anecdote shared, or from the author exchanges between Joy and Kami.

The following action steps are for anyone interested in

understanding feminist history and your role in it. However, they might be most useful to diversity officers, coaches, human resource teams, and other leaders/activists in diversity and inclusion initiatives. It's helpful to start with your own experiences with feminism and then move beyond to your organization's implementation of feminist key issues and practices. Invoke the guidance of other feminist thought leaders who have done the heavy lifting and use their work to support your arguments.

> Review the brief history of feminism at the beginning of the chapter. Was anything new to you? If so, how has it changed your perspective?

> Read the author exchange between Kami and Joy in this chapter. Consider your own response to the question. How did you arrive to feminism? If you haven't yet, what's stopping you?

> How can you apply your knowledge of feminist movements to changes that need to be made within your organization? How can you help others do so?

> Find two or three feminist scholars, activists, or simply amazing women you have an affinity for but who are also different from you. (We provide some of our favorites in Appendix B.) Read at least one of their books, watch a movie about them, or do some thorough Internet searches, then tell stakeholders what you learned and pass it on. If you are a coach, provide mentorship and mastermind opportunities with your clients. Think about how you would facilitate book clubs and other types of resource sharing. For example, if you feel drawn to womanist scholars, read books by Patricia Hill Collins or

collect poetry by Virginia Brindis de Salas. Find several quotes and actions that they have talked about and implement those in your personal and professional life. Frame the quotes and put them in your workspace as a reminder of this new perspective or new understanding about yourself and others.

CHAPTER 2

The Pervasive Patriarchy

> Sometimes I have to ask myself: at what point will I not
> have to demand to be supported by the white women
> in my department? When will I need to stop reminding
> them to stick up for me when people say things that are
> untrue or offensive? Then I have to remind myself, it
> doesn't stop until they WANT to do it on their own.
>
> —Ashley, 48, African American, professor

Every day, women wake up to a steady stream of input. This input tells us what we should look like, how we should act, and who we need to be in order to survive in the world. It can be subtle, like the number of diet commercials aired during a morning commute, or overt, like being told by a colleague that our tone of voice is intimidating to others and should be altered for collegiality. This daily input permeates every aspect of our lives and seeps into both our individual psyches and our collective understanding of the capabilities of women, including body image and our value as worthy citizens, workers, intellectuals, mothers, partners, and friends. In the workplace, these messages can look and sound like lower pay for equal work, being interrupted by our colleagues while speaking, or being evaluated subjectively (on our personalities) rather than objectively (being evaluated solely on our productivity and skill level).

What's more insidious is that when women begin to believe these lies of inadequacy, they tend to act on those beliefs and treat other women in a negative manner, especially along other social discriminatory lines like race, class, gender, language, ability, and age. How can we break this cycle? We can inspect our privilege and use our power. Privilege and power are the domain in which voices are heard, systems are enacted, and equality depends on those who can wield political, national, corporate, educational, or religious power. Without power and privilege, it's harder to be heard.

What Is Patriarchy?

So, what is patriarchy exactly? You may be familiar with the term, but here's how we understand it. In a patriarchal system, people are unwittingly forced to conform to a system of competitive and cut-throat expectations, a system that, in the Western world, has been based on white male heteronormative practices. This system exemplifies white male values, perpetuates inequality around pay, promotes racism, sexism, and homophobia, and supports continued discrimination against other groups. In his book *How Can I Get Through to You? Closing the Intimacy Gap Between Men and Women*, Terry Real, a senior faculty member at the Family Institute of Cambridge and director of the Gender Relations Program at the Meadows Institute in Arizona, discusses how patriarchy hurts all of us, men and women.[1] Men are meant to be strong, to be the breadwinner and not show emotion or vulnerability. Women should be submissive, weak, and passive. This ideology creates a rift in marriage, friendships, and workplace relationships — clearly, we don't all fit cleanly into boxes. Patriarchy suppresses the opportunity for women to access higher level jobs, and instead of encouraging collaboration, it encourages an unhealthy sort of competition. There are of course exceptions to this, but the underlying foundation of patriarchy is the continued investment in and engagement to it. That's where women come in. Writer bell hooks describes patriarchy as "imperialist white-supremacist capitalist patriarchy," to describe the interlocking political systems that are the basis of our nation's politics.[2] She continues to suggest that patriarchy's political-social system insists that males are inherently dominant and superior. Females are deemed weak and need to be continuously dominated through various forms of psychological terrorism and violence. Religion and politics are some of the major forms of perpetuating patriarchy. Our complicity in and lack of understanding patriarchy is why it continues to have a strong hold over all of us.

Follow us for a moment here. When women sabotage each other, we judge each other just as much as society judges us. We tend to "check" each other according to these societal norms, inclusive of all the stereotypical "feminine" conventions: a small waistline, glowing skin, be soft but not too weak — and God forbid if you present as a strong woman who expresses confidence in her leadership and is rewarded for it. We are told we don't have the right to our own feelings and our anger is not justified.

- -

A Picture of Sabotage

Angie was an ob/gyn in a clinic with two female partners and two male partners. When she announced that she was pregnant with her third child, the news was met with much consternation, especially from her female partners. For her maternity leave she proposed using all of her vacation time for the year and only six of the twelve weeks of available paid short-term disability. She also offered to make up all of the calls that she would have otherwise taken while on maternity leave. She was told by one of her female partners that her colleagues were "not going to pay for her lifestyle decision." She was also told that not only was maternity leave "not in the spirit" of the practice's paid disability policy but that she would have to pay overhead to them while on leave. The resistance to her having any sort of a maternity leave other than leave without pay, while also paying thousands of dollars to her partners for overhead, came almost exclusively from one of the female partners. The other female partner was unsupportive as well and essentially refused to speak with her about the matter. Ironically, she received the most support from one of the male partners, but even he failed to convince the female partners to compromise on their expectations. Eventually she felt she had no choice other than to leave the practice and take a hospital-based position.

· ·

On a daily basis, women experience myriad interactions and situations that support patriarchy more than we may be aware of. There are obvious instances: sexual harassment and assault and rape, for example. There are others that we may not consider. Sexist language, or referencing our gender in many professional titles such as "female CEOs" or "woman engineer," is a way in which we may demonstrate support for patriarchy by inferring that it is not usual or normal to have women in particular positions of power. Additionally, sabotaging actions such as harassment, slut-shaming (acting as if a woman shouldn't own her sexuality), lower pay, policing our tone, language, dress, and personalities, and even judging styles of mothering or whether we choose to not have children, are riddled with patriarchal expectations. Angie's situation above exemplifies how women may sabotage each other even when it seems like they are equal in power, but the structure of patriarchy still sets the stage for sabotage to happen. The need to make money, to not have as much time off because we are expected to work even when family should come first, is all part of a male-dominated structure where the family does not hold equal value. When we witness a man behaving in this way, we rally together and call him on the carpet for disrespecting our sister. But rarely do we step up when we witness a woman do these things to another woman — even though when we act this way toward one another, it seems even more insidious and permeates our everyday experiences. In Angie's case, the male doctor could even see the injustice but did little to stop it.

The Effects of Socialization

Think of the way you were socialized (in terms of gender) while you were growing up. If you are a woman, think back to your junior high and high school years. What were your friendships like? When did you feel supported and when did you feel bullied? What did the bullying look like? Were there taunts about some aspect of you being a girl? We discuss gender identity here because one of the main ways women undermine each other is through body image. Our culture, in which women are sexualized, is evidence of the effects of patriarchal notions. Common narrative holds that women are objects of desire; this based on our bodies, instead of our intellect.

Consider your present tense. Are you and your female friends caught up in dieting, fussing about looking younger or being more sexually desirable? On the flip side, do you shame (or have you shamed) other women for being too promiscuous or for their offbeat sense of style? As you can imagine, these seemingly innocent instances are forms of sabotage.

To help us better understand socialization, we first need to dismantle our social identities and how they have shaped our position in and perspective of the world. Socialization is a life-long process that starts with our families, but also stems from our history and ancestors. Parents and guardians are the first socializers and start with norms, values, and beliefs. This can be as simple as pink or blue, or as deep as calling a young girl a tomboy because she likes to play football and admonishing her for not playing with dolls instead. Depending on how we are socialized by our families, geographic region, or other cultural practices around gender norms, we might be praised for following the status quo and punished when we rebel or question social norms. For example, in Joy's teacher education classes, she asks her students why they want to become teachers. Some answers include, "I was told that I was good with children and my mom was a teacher," "I liked school and my parents thought I would be a good teacher," or "I thought that would be the only thing I would be good at, but now I'm wondering if I could have chosen something I'm actually interested in rather than choosing something I was told suited me because I am a girl." Many sociologists and communication theorists describe socialization with the term "social construct."[3] It explains how all of our interactions within society develop and shape our understandings of the world. These understandings then form the basis for shared assumptions about reality through thoughts, behaviors, and norms. Put simply: we know the world based on who we interact with regularly. A sociologist would likely argue that *everything* is a social construct: race, gender, sexuality, age, and even time. It's crucial to think through the many socializing influences of your culture in your life. This is important work, so you can get a grasp of how they reinforce and reshape each other.

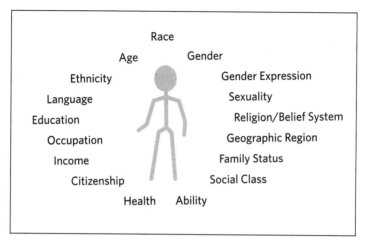

Race

Age   Gender

Ethnicity   Gender Expression

Language   Sexuality

Education   Religion/Belief System

Occupation   Geographic Region

Income   Family Status

Citizenship   Social Class

Health   Ability

Figure 1: Social constructions of identity

Figure 1 shows a visual that may be helpful.

How might we deconstruct or take apart our upbringing to illuminate the areas in which we have experienced both privilege and discrimination? How might the socialization of the world's expectations of us seep into our subconscious? We use the term "internalized oppression" to define putting stock in the noisy stories around you — those of not belonging, or being unable to connect, when the voice in your head tells you you're not good enough. We work to unmask these voices for what they are, the voices of a society steeped in oppression and discrimination. In order to build the skills necessary for repairing and healing internalized oppression, we can start by observing the origins of our thoughts. In chapter 3, we'll lead you through some exercises that aid the process of deconstructing what we think we know about who we are. Often, women of color, including Kami, are overtly treated with (or wonder if their treatment is due to) racist assumptions of their competence compared to their white peers. Across the board, women struggle with a deep-seated self-doubt. How can we "flip the script" internally so we can demand the world see us differently? As you read our stories, think through your own socialization. Where do you want to begin to rewrite your story?

Women in Leadership

The hashtag #banbossy is all about girls embracing their ability to be the boss and not letting other people tell them they are bossy.[4] When a woman is in charge, the perception is that there's a fine line between being too bossy or too harsh. Catalyst conducted a study evaluating a woman's ability to lead in effective ways.[5] They saw that even though there are more women leaders in some organizations, it doesn't necessarily mean that an individual woman will be evaluated fairly. When Joy, for example, asked for a raise, she was called "forceful," even though she was asking for a fair wage. According to Catalyst, men are usually evaluated on their productivity statistics and not their personality. We have talked to countless women who suggest their evaluations were based on their personalities, rather than their productivity. Adjectives such as abrupt, abrasive, too nice, not nice, and even sassy are frequently used. Christina, a public relations specialist we interviewed for this book, was told as she was leaving her job, "You've been a real asset to the department and we're sorry to see you go, but you were also a little sassy." Another woman we spoke to, Harriet, was taken aside by her boss and told, "You are being too abrasive; your employees are not happy." We have many examples: after listening to one of our presentations, another woman told us that she was told she was being "too nice" and that she wasn't being taken seriously by her colleagues. This might feel like a double bind; as women, we can't be too abrasive or too nice, too honest or a pushover. We're told that to be a strong leader we must be assertive, make hard decisions, and have few "friends." But we are also told indirectly, most of the time, that we have to watch how we speak to our colleagues to not appear abrasive. This is a fine balance we seem obligated to maintain. In her research, Kim Elsesser, psychologist and gender theorist at the Center for Study of Women at UCLA, found that women actually preferred male bosses because they don't backbite like other women do.[6] She indicated that the rift in leadership between men and women stems from discomfort and anxiety around networking, social events, and the distinction between friendliness and sexual harassment.

200 Percent

If you have friends or colleagues of color, especially black women, you've probably heard the following: you have to perform 200 percent better than your white peers and there will still *always* be a question of your competence (more colloquially, this theory is phrased as "twice as good for half as much"). When Kami was growing up, this notion was unspoken within many conversations with family, friends, and the influential black adults in her life. Often, it is a force that is never named outside the safe spaces occupied by black individuals.

This particular type of socialization sticks with black people the most. Even at their best they may still not be good enough, even though they have put in more effort, more sweat, more blood, and far more tears (likely in the dark when no one is watching) in order to make it in this world.

You can imagine this is a lot of pressure for a child, especially because they'll carry this weight for the rest of their lives. In Kami's case, no one ever explicitly had this conversation with her, save for subtle references — like when she came home crying after a teacher accused her of cheating when she aced a test, saying, "You couldn't have done that well on your own," or when she was told by a guidance counselor to "just stick to state school" even though she was a high performer and was offered full-ride scholarships. Kami was told she wouldn't make it at Spelman because it was statistically "impossible" that she would succeed. For Kami, and for other women who have had similar experiences, socialization means defying odds as the product of a teen mother in the inner city of an urban Midwestern area and obtaining her Ph.D. It means being mothered by a woman who exposed her child to wide cross-sections of art, from chamber music to Toni Morrison, Stephen King to Virginia Hamilton. Socialization tells us this woman could not have entered into a committed, monogamous relationship built on respect. Socialization means this woman has an ability to flutter between cultures, because she is unable to be her authentic self in all situations. However, for Kami and perhaps for others like her, socialization also includes getting "poor child" glances from those in positions of privilege and power, or having kids of your home culture shun you, while having kids of the dominant culture keep you close only as an advantage and only on their terms. We don't mean to diminish the struggles white women have had in the workplace, especially when it comes to fighting for equal standing with male counterparts. But for black women, and many women of color, the 200 percent "rule" is an added weight. These women will always wonder if they are being judged on two levels: for their gender as well as their ethnic or cultural representation.

W. E. B. Du Bois and Double Consciousness

In his book, *The Souls of Black Folk*, W. E. B. Du Bois coined the term "double consciousness," which he explains as "the sense of always looking at one's self through the eyes of others, of measuring one's soul by the tape of the world that looks on in amused contempt and pity."[7] This is a heavy burden on black people because it is no doubt intersectionality. But it is also unmistakably difficult, arduous without fail, and unrelentingly heavy.

We believe that for black women, socialization is involved in this notion of double consciousness. For Kami, although her mother gave her all the tools she needed to be black and proud, feminine, confident, and the consummate achiever, she still struggles with the perceptions about black women in the workplace, and worries about being seen first for her blackness, instead of her ability.

Socialization and Double Consciousness: The Other Side of the Coin

Not every white woman fits into the patriarchy's ideal of what a woman should be. Plenty of women, of color or not, claim many identities — single, partnered, with children, without children, queer, nonbinary, any myriad of others. When Joy was a young girl, she was bombarded with the constructs surrounding white female identity. Although she moved around a lot — the consequences of being born into a military family — the southern Texas values of how a proper young lady should look and act were well indoctrinated. Be pretty, nice, demure, and rely on men to be chivalrous.

She had the usual complement of "girl" toys (even though one of her Barbies had a data processing center, she still had this Barbie processing data on a little boy named Sherman). For her, the message was clear: men and boys are in power and in order to survive, you need to find one to take care of you; however, you are secretly the boss in powerful positions like in the kitchen and with the children. Your man is to take care of you, adore you, but that's in exchange for the burden you bear not being fully actualized as a human being.

It didn't take Joy long to realize the differences in the ways her classmates of color were treated compared to her and her white classmates. After returning to Texas from living in Germany for a while, she learned quickly that black people were not treated the same, and women were to be respectful of their men, quiet, pretty, and skinny. The globalized way of living she had adopted during the family's stint in Germany came to a screeching halt. During these school years, her personal expectation was that she would follow a traditional path: get a teaching degree, find a (white) man, get married, have a baby, remain a teacher and ensure a good work/life balance, be a good mother and wife. Better be good to your man and keep him interested, because he is your lifeline. If he cheats, forgive him, but by all means, don't let him walk away no matter what. Our young girls and women continue to be socialized in this way, and when they don't fit into that mold, it can cause significant trauma, as it did for Joy — because her life didn't follow this neatly laid-out plan. Instead, she barely got into college, and, once there, she quit her sorority based on the way she saw women of color being treated during rush week. She pierced her belly button and nose, and generally behaved in a way that put her out of the running for that traditional lifestyle her socialization so desperately laid out for her. All the while, she squelched her queerness as life progressed — through to Arizona, into Washington State, her obtaining of her master's and doctoral degrees, failed marriages, a child. Finally, she was able to accept herself and come out to her family, and step out on her own path. We share Joy's story of socialization and experience with patriarchy for this reason.

During a recent conversation with a young white woman, Joy learned that at this woman's workplace there had been a lot of backbiting and outward fighting among the female colleagues. She said her new male boss put a stop to it, and the women were finally able to work in peace. She said he was kind of a dad figure and he even calls himself the "work dad." However, to Joy the scene was reminiscent of a brood of hens being put in their place by the rooster. Joy asked this woman, "Why do you think this work dad was needed? Do you think the women in your office could have handled the backbiting on their own? And do you think you all had ingrained in you this idea that only a man could fix the meddling hens?" The look on this woman's face suggested she hadn't even thought about that. It's a great example of how the patriarchy continues. Our goal is to kick out the rooster, free the hens, burn the coop down, and create an equitable free-range cooperative where all chickens have equal access. And while the previous statement is intentionally hyperbolic, these seemingly small "aha" moments are what start the revolution.

· ·

AUTHOR EXCHANGE
On Patriarchy

This chapter talks about the ways in which we have been socialized and how that has shaped our perception and view of the world. We argue that patriarchy is a system that is contributing to how we sabotage one another. We feel it is important to share how Joy and Kami were socialized through patriarchy. Through transparency and vulnerability, this exchange between Joy and Kami will show how "smashing the patriarchy" is a work in progress, but absolutely possible.

Joy

In my early adolescence and up to my early twenties, even though I couldn't name patriarchy, I could sense it, feel it, and witnessed it on a daily basis. The naming of it would elude me for at least another ten years. The only part of patriarchy that was clear and somewhat nameable was when I would walk the halls of the army base, where masculinity was a dense fog full of salutes, uniforms, buzz cuts, and stern faces. There were a few officers who smiled at me because they knew my dad, but other than that, they scared the bejesus out of me. I have always been well aware of my not-enoughness, my intangible lack of self-confidence, and that's why I settled — for forty years — for what I thought I could manage to do, rather than what I really wanted to do. I didn't listen to my intuition and didn't think I could actually achieve what I wanted. Like Kami, I also thought I could trick men into loving me by being someone I'm not. I clutched so tightly to the Prince Charming narrative that I inadvertently choked the life right out of myself.

In school, it was made very clear that the white boys got to be in honors classes, they were allowed to take up space to show off their smarts or even to behave badly, and they seemed confident in doing so. The message I received was that I was to be passive, quiet, and get by — thriving didn't seem like an option. (In later years, experience taught me that boys suffered under patriarchy too; the only deep emotion they are allowed to express is anger.)

I somehow have always known that we all suffer under patriarchy's quest for top-down power dynamics, competition, greed, and lust for power *over*, rather than power *with*. Collaboration, vulnerability, trust, and equitable access to opportunities of all kinds, be it within the workplace, sports, places of worship, classrooms, or anywhere else, are sometimes only available in a few quiet, relatively safe, and cloistered spaces where patriarchy hasn't reached out its formidable grasp.

Kami

Despite attempts to demonstrate that she was a "strong black woman" (and she was), my mother has always been keen on the Prince Charming narrative. She wanted to be whisked away to Happily Ever After to create the ideal two-parent household, the loving environment that she missed in her own childhood. Thus, this ideal has been ingrained in my psyche. When she had me, I think she felt she was continuing a life she didn't want, as my own father was not there for my childhood. There was a constant pull between independence and dependence on the patriarchal system that she may or may not have even realized. And then, despite the wonderful womanist work that my undergraduate experience afforded me, there were still undertones of the Southern belle identity. My classmates and I were brilliant, independent, young black women thinkers who still needed to be protected by the male forces around us. We were given brothers from neighboring Morehouse College, who were responsible for our safety and well-being after dark.

In fact, I think the Prince Charming narrative has been in the back of my conscious mind, dictating how I interacted with men, engaged my own femininity and womanliness, and contributed to the sabotage of others. The more I consider the question of patriarchy, the more I realize I have to acknowledge my own role in how I perpetuate it, even in the midst of my womanist worldview.

Utilizing patriarchy is actually how I sabotaged. As a teenager, I actively engaged in slut-shaming to keep my male friends from dating particular girls in the class. I played the damsel in distress to keep certain boyfriends in college. I made snide comments about my father's infidelity around my mother, thinking I was "helping" when really I was just rehashing her pain. These contradictions are necessary to share because I claim to be "antipatriarchy." But sabotage is my saying this while still holding on to the parts of patriarchy that benefit *me*. In this regard, I am definitely a work in progress. I have moved on from many behaviors, like slut-shaming or rehashing the pain of other women. However, I cling to the notion of the damsel in distress. Although I may no longer do it to "keep" a partner, there are ways in which I rely on it to get help instead of just asking for it. I have pity parties about my poor life in order to get folks to stop focusing on themselves and save me and my issues. Yes. This *is* patriarchy. Why? Even though I may not discriminate about who I get the help from, man or woman, I'm still seeking someone else to save "poor little princess" me so I don't have to be held accountable for my own issues. Sabotage is admonishing patriarchy while still benefiting from it, no matter how nondiscriminant you make the packaging. Support is turning to other women, like Joy, and asking them to hold me accountable when they see me slipping into habit. I'm still battling patriarchy — but not just on the outside alongside other women. I'm battling the patriarchy within too.

• •

Action Steps

Take a moment to work through the following questions. If you're leading a diversity and inclusion (D&I) group, for example, or reading this as part of a workplace book group, feel free to recast them to suit your individual situation.

› What is your experience with patriarchy, and what does it mean to you? How much do you know about this word and its systemic influence? How have you been advantaged and disadvantaged by it?

› Think through each cultural influence in your life: where you were raised, the type of school you attended, the type of religious institution you were a part of, your first toys, your family's views on social norms such as gender, and so on. How have your race, gender identity, class, age, geographic region, language, ethnicity, and ability shaped the opportunities you received and didn't receive? For instance, how did your race affect the schools you went to and the way you were treated in school? How did the convergence of race and gender affect the experiences you had in schooling, your access to health care, engagement with media, and socialization within your community? It will be helpful to write this down.

› Identify statements made in the workplace that infer women of color are victims of unfortunate circumstances. Can you point to evidence that these statements are based in fact? If not, speak up and correct these statements as they are made.

› Compare Du Bois's explanation of double consciousness to Crenshaw's explanation of intersectionality, as discussed in chapter 1. Identify how these two concepts manifest in your black women peers at work.

> Let your knowledge of "200 percent better" allow you to offer empathy and understanding to black women. Ask yourself, is she saying yes because she *wants* to do this or because she feels she *has* to do this? Have I done or said anything to make her feel as though she has to do what I am asking even if she does not actually have the bandwidth?

CHAPTER 3

The Power of Privilege

> My authentic self would be more vulnerable, both in taking risks with program development and in connecting on a more human level with my colleagues. I'd move through my work days feeling more confident, creative, and playful. I'd feel respected for my quiet contributions to the workplace.
>
> —Audrey, white, 34, program coordinator
> in higher education

*A*s individuals, we may stand as one person, but we represent our ancestors and our history, and that legacy trickles down to us, the descendants. Whenever she leads workshops and trainings, Kami asks participants to consider every single role they hold personally, professionally, and socially. In doing so, she allows them to understand that in any given moment, those roles may be prioritized and ranked in order to reflect the interaction, but they never truly go away. For example, the Salvadoran female colleague who may speak on the phone to her Spanish-only mother in a hushed voice at work to not be overheard, or the Muslim female colleague who just appears antisocial when not joining the department for lunch during Ramadan because she doesn't want to tell you she's in the middle of a fasting season for her religion. We have many roles and many ways to see ourselves. It's important to know that when we are relating to another person, we are not just an individual relating to another individual. We are many.

When Joy leads workshops, she uses her own family tree as a teaching tool. Her great-great-grandfather was a Texas Ranger; his son, Joy's great-grandfather, was a doctor, and his son, Joy's grandfather, was a NATO officer; finally, his son, Joy's father, held a doctorate degree, became a Green Beret and a medic in the army, and served in the Vietnam War. This lineage of white male privilege and education paved the way for Joy's own education and the other opportunities she has enjoyed in life. All this to say, our existence isn't formed in a vacuum. Our access to life's possibilities is not always equal. Acknowledging privilege is so integral to understanding how we are positioned in the world in very particular ways that give us both privilege and marginalization.

In this chapter, we will take you through how we function with our various converging identities. With these identities, there are personal stories that emerged from our interactions in society which connect together to create who we are. Many times, it's very clear what the story is; we might even call it a script that was handed to us. It could be the way we were conditioned to move through the world as women, where we were clear we had to be beautiful, nice, and quiet. Other times, the story is a little muddy, where we weren't quite sure how to fit in or if we even wanted to.

Here, we will confront the stories or scripts connected to race, gender, and other identities so we can begin to understand the many ways we walk through the world and are perceived by it. In doing so, we can better understand how women are sometimes socialized to tear each other down along these lines of privilege and marginalization.

We can begin by looking at race. Race is also not a siloed entity — two people of the same race may have wildly different experiences. However, as Crenshaw described, women of color, particularly black women, have very different experiences than white women. Both Joy and Kami will describe our experiences more in depth later in the chapter.

Through the Lens of Race

As we mentioned, Joy was privileged to have experiences with a wide variety of people and to have parents who believed that interacting with and respecting different cultures was important. However, that doesn't mean that she and her family didn't benefit from white privilege and didn't hold racist attitudes. Whether her family knew it or not, they benefited from walking around in stores without fear of being followed, or being late to a meeting and not having their lateness chalked up to their race. If we look through the lens of white privilege, we can see how some are paid more due to their race and given more unquestioned access to opportunities. As a student, Joy went to good schools; she saw herself in her white teachers, the literature she read, the movies she watched, and the other white students in her honors classes. When moving into a new neighborhood, Joy's family could be pretty sure they wouldn't be received negatively based on their race.

POWER STRUCTURES

Joy has held enough workshops to know there is always one white person who says, "But I can't go into a black neighborhood and feel welcome." That person may or may not be right, but let's examine this a bit closer. Figure 2 describes some types of institutional and structural power and racism:

- **Structural racism.** History and current reality of oppression across institutions combined to create a

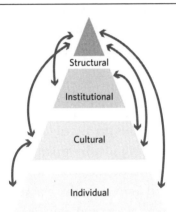

Structural Racism: History and current reality of oppression across institutions combined to create a system of oppression that trickles down from the top (i.e., white supremacist, patriarchal, capitalist, heteronormative systems that keep white men in power)

Institutional Racism: Policies: and procedures to provide advantages to whites and barriers for POC (anti-blackness, school to prison to deportation pipeline, mass incarceration/detention, war on terror and Islamophobia, anti-Muslim travel ban)

Cultural Racism: At its core is a form of racism that relies on cultural differences rather than on biological markers of superiority or inferiority through language, art, images, material objects, ideas, and rituals.

Individual Racism: Individual acts (explicit and implicit bias)

The structure (white supremacy, patriarchy) creates the institutional (health care, educational, legal, economic, and political), which gets reinforced by cultural practices shown in media. This then informs and affects the way we navigate our personal and professional relationships and dynamics. In the media, white men are shown as the CEOs and decision makers at home, at work, in politics, and other forms of power, whereas women and people of color are relegated to the sidelines. This affects how we see ourselves as leaders and change makers. If we don't see ourselves in power, it's harder to imagine that we can change the status quo.

Figure 2: Types of power and racism

system of oppression that trickles down from the top (i.e., white supremacist, patriarchal, capitalist, heteronormative system that keeps white men in power).

- **Institutional racism.** Policies and procedures to provide advantages to whites and barriers for people of color (anti-blackness, school to prison to deportation pipeline, mass incarceration/detention, war on terror and Islamophobia, anti-Muslim travel ban).

- **Cultural racism.** At its core, a form of racism that relies on cultural differences rather than on biological markers of superiority or inferiority through language, art, images, material objects, ideas, and rituals.

- **Individual racism.** Individual acts (explicit and implicit bias).

Frequently there is an abundance of representation of the white race in leadership roles in institutions like health care, legal systems, politics, and education. These institutions dictate policies and laws that directly or indirectly prohibit certain groups of people in poverty from getting access to services they would otherwise have. When we see the systemic effects of white supremacy on the institutions, we are able to see the larger picture of institutionalized and systemic oppression around race. Certainly it's no coincidence that those most affected by poverty are people of color and other people who come from generations of poverty. Perhaps a white person is in the minority in their neighborhood or at an event, but they are not the minority when it comes to the various forms of real power. It's very important to understand the difference here. Systemic power is a lot more powerful than everyday situations. However, until people in those everyday situations start to take a real look at how power is being wielded based on systemic racism, then nothing will really change. It's a cyclical pattern. When we add in gender and other converging identities, the situation becomes even more nuanced and complex.

Within educational institutions, where a lot of socialization perpetuates inequity and feeds external and internalized oppression, what are the qualities of those in power — for example, the superintendents or board of trustees? If you work for a corporate institution, does your organization have a diversity and inclusion team? When we start to look at how institutional power trickles down from the top, and affects institutions like education, employment, criminal justice, health care, social services, government, and other entities, we can see how it seeps down to our cultural norms and then to individual daily interactions.

....

Flint, Michigan, and Institutionalized Racism

A good example of institutionalized racism is the water crisis in Flint, Michigan. For three years, African American citizens complained that people in their communities were getting sick. It was discovered that thousands of Flint residents, many of them children, were exposed to dangerous levels of lead with the support of government corruption. As this book is being written, residents of Flint, Michigan, have been living for more than 1,500 days on bottled water for their safety. Putting communities of color in danger by ignoring their complaints has been common practice for years in regard to access to health care, clean and affordable housing, and safe and high-functioning schools. The surrounding white communities were getting clear and uncontaminated water. This situation makes institutional and environmental racism clear. A history of structural and systemic racism combined with implicit bias was a large part of why no one did anything about Flint's water crisis until much too late.[1]

. . . .

EDUCATION AND SOCIALIZATION

As we discussed in the previous chapter, our educational system is the most influential when it comes to socialization.[2] Teacher education programs are continually trying to diversify the teaching force by moving away from the majority — white female teachers — to include more people of color and men. Even so, Joy, who has worked in teacher education for twenty years, has witnessed the continued similitude of our nation's teachers; they remain primarily middle-class, young white females. This can be chalked up to a variety of reasons, based largely around social constructions (the common narrative dictates this career choice is best suited for women from that background), but we can also extrapolate that students of color didn't see themselves in their teacher's faces. On top of that, they may have had bad experiences in the education system. Why would they then want to pursue such a job?

There are many explanations for why the teaching force remains relatively homogeneous. Aforementioned teacher education programs are trying to recruit a diverse array of teachers, but many times these programs reflect the current educational system, which still embodies white male heteronormative, monolingual policies and practices, specifically in the way history is taught and from whose perspective.[3] Additionally, research shows that children of color and children in poverty are disproportionately penalized.[4] As Django Paris notes, "Deficit approaches to teaching and learning, firmly in place prior to and during the 1960s and 1970s, viewed the languages, literacies, and cultural ways of being of many students and communities of color as deficiencies to be overcome in learning the demanded and legitimized dominant language, literacy, and cultural ways of schooling."[5]

What does all of this have to do with privilege and sabotage? When the beginnings of our K–12 experience reflect the socialization of predominantly white teachers, diverse perspectives and cultural experiences become invalidated and marginalized.

Deconstruct What You Think You Know

We've talked about social constructions in chapter 2, and dipped into it a bit more in this chapter. To put a fine point on it, we can think about social constructions as the scaffolding around a building. Each message we receive is a board or ladder used to construct the building — in this case, *you*. Think about the early messages you received about your gender, race, age, ability, sexual orientation, ethnicity, socioeconomic class, and/or language. When did you first start to notice what it meant to be a girl or boy? Who told you what was acceptable and what wasn't? Who told you who was acceptable to marry? Did you consistently see examples of your race in the faces of people who had power over you, such as teachers, supervisors, or youth leaders? To deconstruct means to take apart those early messages and the continuing narrative or story about those messages — as scaffolding around a building is temporary, so can be the way we are socialized.

Socialization doesn't mean life is without choice. It does mean we may be heavily influenced by societal and cultural expectations. Unless we start to examine cultural practices, we may be subjected to unintentionally following a prescribed script. We liken this to characters in a play, given scripts before birth detailing the place, time, and social identity they came into the world with. The script, as written, began with external messages internalized by the characters until they eventually began to believe those messages were true. But as they begin to play out that script, they also begin to question it.

To deconstruct these social constructs is to examine their origin and their validity in who you believe you truly are. That might be your authentic self, trusting your intuition about how you walk through the world and who you want to be. It involves a constant interrogation of the messages you receive from the global society, the people around you, and even yourself.

In order to deconstruct, we begin by addressing our internal narrative loops, those thoughts, assumptions, ideas, opinions, judgments, and layers of social commentary that often turn into statements and actions that perpetuate bias, prejudice, and stereotyping. When we internalize these messages, they can take the form of the imposter syndrome — the idea that we don't belong or we aren't worthy. Using the social identity model from chapter 2 (see figure 1), and through examples, we examine where that messaging might have come from in our lives. We can then start to examine how we judge others. Until we take a deep dive into the deconstruction of our socializations, we can't begin to deconstruct what we think of others.

IMPOSTER SYNDROME AFFECTS THE BEST OF US

Joy grew up thinking that she wasn't smart enough to go to college, and once she was in, she still didn't believe she really belonged. Even after she made it to her doctoral program, she felt like it was a fluke that she got in and that at some point someone would unveil the truth: that she really wasn't smart enough to be in graduate school and that she was a fraud. For Kami, despite the fact her grades, intellect, and wit showed she deserved to be in every advanced placement and honors class she took — and was the best candidate for every single award and accolade she received — there is always a nagging voice that whispers, "They just needed to have a black person to be nice. It's not your worth, it's their need for 'diversity.' You were just their safest bet for the gamble." Most women — most people — experience this type of negative self-talk, which holds us back and may cause us to react to others in less than savory ways. In order to break these thought loops, we must constantly work to interrupt them. We also need to look at how we judge others based on our social constructions.

Checking Our Privilege

Let's take a moment to examine how privilege and marginalization have shaped the way we see ourselves in certain positions of power such as manager of a team, chair of an academic department, or executive in the C-suite. We'll examine our understanding of who we are and the cultural groups we belong to, and why it's necessary to continuously question how these groups shape how we see and think about the "-isms" in our society.

From current discussions around privilege, it is a relatively safe assumption to associate the word "privilege" with the concept of "white privilege." However, much like with our discussion about sabotage, reducing the term "privilege" to encapsulate only white privilege prevents us from seeing the privileges that we actually have even in the midst of what we may feel is oppression. To illustrate this perspective, Kami offers her viewpoint as a black woman.

PRIVILEGE: A DIFFERENT PERSPECTIVE

Looking solely at the sociocultural history of blacks in America, it would be logical to guess that Kami has very little privilege. The history of mistreatment, systemic oppression, and discrimination against black people shows that privilege is not usually associated with her racial group. But if you layer other aspects of Kami's story, look at her family history and lived experience, any assumption made about her lack of privilege would be incorrect.

To be clear, we can't suggest that Kami is, or has been, afforded the same opportunities that come with whiteness. It's important to acknowledge that despite some of the disadvantages imposed on black people there are still some privileges that many can claim. One of those privileges is education. Kami is the child of a single parent; in this case, we need to remember the common narrative associated with black single mothers (it doesn't typically involve the mother holding two degrees — one advanced — as Kami's mother does). Because Kami's mother is educated, access to education was stacked in her daughter's favor, so it's not surprising that Kami herself holds a Ph.D. If this makes sense to you, it shows that having even one parent with an advanced degree makes it more likely that their children will obtain the same. Additionally, many black children have been pushed to outdo their parents when it comes to education, career, and quality of life (Kami can certainly relate to this). For black women, this is especially important to understand. Not because this affords them the degree of privilege afforded our white sisters, but because it gives them a degree of privilege within their blackness among others of their racial group — the same can be said for a woman of any marginalized group: Latina, Asian, indigenous. With this degree of privilege, it's possible that women of these groups may have at some point sabotaged one of their own, because those other women may not have had the same educational privilege.

This form of sabotage may be evidenced in the act of cutting another woman down because she doesn't have a college degree, or bypassing her application because her degree comes from a community college — a perceived "lesser" institution. Kami admits to being guilty of this. But she's come to understand that because she has this privilege, she needs to engage differently in order to offer support to other women. Kami needs to accept that, yes, a woman can choose not to go to college, and it's not a measure of her intelligence. It's possible a woman of color may desire to advance her education but is challenged by obstacles in her path. Instead of dismissing that woman, Kami can talk to her, and discover if that woman has a desire to forward her education, and if there's anything Kami can do to remove at least some of those obstacles. Kami can give this woman space to accept (or not) the privileges she was afforded through education.

Power as a Tool for Sabotage

Power holds a significant influence on the maintenance of the systemic oppressions, discriminations, and biases we face. Power regulates who has access, who can achieve, who can govern, and who can run a corporation. Women of color have certainly felt the advantages and disadvantages of power in our professional lives. Women in general have used power as a tool for sabotage. The experiences that come from using power as a tool for advancement, protection, and in some cases sabotage often make it difficult for us to easily identify our privileges. Let's unpack this with a brief case study.

POWER: A CASE STUDY

Beverly was promoted to a senior vice president role with her banking firm. In this new role, she would be responsible for performance evaluations of middle managers and also for their professional growth and development. The promotion was an opportunity for Beverly to show the other senior VPs that she knew this organization well; she could read people and have a positive impact on the growth of the company through productivity plans. She was ready. Over several weeks, she had looked at the past evaluations of all of the middle managers. She identified strengths and weaknesses; she pored over workshops and seminars that she could offer as suggestions to the managers to improve their weaker areas. This was her moment to show the organization she was a team player, diligent and detailed.

Amy was a middle manager who worked well with her team, but the team as a whole weren't overachievers. They all did their jobs well; they were actively engaged in cross-team projects, they submitted all their reports on time, and all of their evaluations were positive. Beverly saw an opportunity to push Amy to be more assertive and show that she was hungry to succeed. When Beverly sat down with Amy to discuss her performance, she told Amy she needed to work on being "too nice" and suggested she immediately enroll in effective communication courses to be more assertive as a manager and attend workshops about how to have difficult conversations in the workplace.

While this may look like a supervisor looking out for her

employee, it's really a power issue. The sabotage is clear and likely a form of unconscious bias; it may be clearer still if you know Beverly is white and Amy is Asian American. Would your perceptions change if both women were black, or of the same racial identity? If Beverly had approached Amy and said instead, "Your team is doing great, but I see you and your team as a big source of untapped potential. As your manager, how can I help you, or inspire you, to inspire your team and push them beyond where they are now?" would it have gone over a bit better? How might Beverly reexamine her perception of Asian American women? This is a great example of learning more about the Asian American experience and the biases they face in the workplace. The Asian American experience isn't a monolithic one; there are many different identities that can fall under this term: Pacific Islander, Filipinx, Taiwanese, Chinese, Korean, Japanese, Thai, Indonesian, and others. They all have different experiences that lead to particular stereotypes and barriers.

THE INTERSECTION OF POWER AND CULTURE

Power is almost inevitably viewed through a cultural lens. When we add the layers of intersectionality and converging identities, and look at power through a race, gender, and class lens, this lens quickly transforms to a kaleidoscope changing into any given shape at any given time. As women we can agree that men have power. But can we also agree that sometimes white women are given power over women of color by men? Can we see that Asian American women are sometimes given power over other women of color? Can we see that how we use our power can either sabotage or support the women around us depending on how we turn our kaleidoscopes before we wield that power? Oftentimes as women we overlook the impact of our power because of its comparison to the power of men. Part of deconstructing how we have been socialized to view power is to no longer view male power as the baseline. When we contextualize our positions of power in the workplace according to not only our rank in the hierarchy but the social positions as well, we start to understand the kaleidoscope can be manipulated along many lines of difference.

••

AUTHOR EXCHANGE
On Intersectionality

Here, Joy and Kami discuss how they individually reflect on the ways they move through the world with both privilege and discrimination. They consider what intersectionality means to each other, and how they can support each other better within their many intersectionalities.

Kami

Sometimes the ways in which intersectionality influences me are a bit comical. For example, when I think of intersectionality and my life, I think about Spike Lee's 1992 movie *Malcolm X*. At the closing credits, he shows a montage of children in classrooms popping up out of their school desks to stand proudly and say "I am Malcolm X!" It's a powerful sequence, which many people missed in the film's theatrical release.

I consider myself one of the people Crenshaw was talking about when she crafted her theory on intersectionality. I am black, I am woman, I am American, I am mother, I am professional, I am wife, I am bilingual. And even though I may be the picture of intersectionality, it doesn't mean I can't and shouldn't reflect on it. It all ties into privilege. My privilege may not look the same as Joy's, but there are some commonalities. We know my mother prioritized my education, which gave me an advantage over youth who did and do not have an opportunity for higher education. It affords me jobs that someone having only a high school diploma cannot attain. It provides me literally more opportunity than many of the folks on my block. Which brings me to socioeconomics.

Regardless of whether the middle class may be more lower middle class in some spots, upper middle class in others, it is still middle class. There is so much privilege in the middle class! We can posture whatever arguments we choose about whether there is really a "true" middle class, but the fact remains, we have one, and we reap a great deal of benefits from society compared to those who may be of a lower socioeconomic rank.

Joy

To me, intersectionality is understanding how black women's voices have been sidelined and systemically silenced again and again — especially now as the term is being co-opted to represent "diverse experiences." How can I support women of color? I know what it's like to feel dismissed and unheard as a queer woman, so I can tap into that experience when someone is sharing similar experiences of dismissiveness. I may not completely relate to it, but I know that I can use my positions of privilege to dismantle the power plays that happen on a daily basis. For instance, when I realize that another woman is being interrupted or not heard, I can use my voice to bring the focus back to what she has said. I can say, "Excuse me, I believe Kami had a great point here..." I can use my privilege as a white person to talk to other white people about racism. I can use my position as a professor in teacher education to interrupt biased actions and words from my students. I can use my privilege to continually seek to understand how my impact in the world is affecting others and call other white people on the carpet to do the same.

Deep down I was always aware of my white privilege, but didn't know exactly how to frame it or understand how I could change it — or if I wanted to change it. But I knew that my whiteness gave me advantages from an early age. I could see how I was treated differently in the classroom when cast next to a black girl in Ms. Lane's third grade classroom. I remember Leticia and how she was treated compared to me by my white teacher. I remember being in middle school and having a sweet friend named Jay whom I really connected with and enjoyed immensely, but when he asked to call me at home I knew that not only would my parents not allow it because he was a boy but more so because he was black.

When I am confronted with my white privilege, I try to flip the script a bit. When a person of color tells me a story of their experience, I try to imagine the times I've felt discriminated against based on my gender and sexual orientation. For example, during a dismantling racism workshop a woman of color told me that, as a white woman, I could go into the middle of a riot where police batons were drawn and ask where the local Starbucks was and get excellent directions. She said black women have been positioned as dangerous, angry, and loose cannons. I wanted to object, I wanted to say, "I would be scared and I don't like going up to a police officer." However, I kept quiet because I knew she was probably right about being white and talking with police officers. I thought of trying to make a man understand why I didn't feel comfortable walking alone at night after work or why calling a woman crazy is deeply problematic. I know there is a history around women being attacked at night or being shut away in mental institutions for being too emotional or outspoken, just like the woman in the above example knows there's a history with black people and police brutality. So when I feel the need to object or defend or shut down when being told about my privilege, I flip the script and imagine how it feels when I am sharing my experience that someone else might not understand.

As a queer woman, I have been told that I don't look like I'm gay or that maybe I'm just "confused" or haven't found the right man. It's infuriating that people feel the need to constantly comment on an aspect of my identity that took me so long to reconcile and be proud of, and secondly, to treat me as if my relationship status is indicative of not only my sexuality but its validity. No one asks a single heterosexual woman if she's sure she's straight. They may say, "Maybe you like women," but if she says no, they are likely to believe her. Bisexual women can experience dismissiveness in both heteronormative and homosexual spaces. Many times I have experienced people questioning if I'm really bisexual just because I'm not in a relationship. As Kami and I have said, intersectionality is about power and privilege, but it also needs to be recentered on black women's experiences, as Kimberlé Crenshaw intended. I am better able to lean in to another perspective if I tap into my own experiences of dismissiveness or discrimination.

·····················

Action Steps

This chapter introduced you to the myriad ways that privilege plays a part in our personal and professional lives. These action steps ask you to examine your socialization based on your cultural identity. How did your family, schooling, and external social messages on race, gender, and class (among others) inform your educational pursuits, current occupation, family life, and social position? How might your experiences have been different if you were of a different race, ethnicity, class, gender, or even in a different geographic location?

> Think through your own family tree. What is the history of your family? What privileges and points of discrimination fed your story, for you to end up where you are right now? Think through the socialization exercise from chapter 2.

> Take a look at the people in power at your organization. What do they look like? How many people of color are represented in the highest echelons of your organization? If you find noticeable gaps in representation, is there a diversity officer or equal employment opportunity (EEO) officer that you can bring these concerns to? If you are in a position to make changes through hiring, what is one change you can make to your hiring process that can expand your pool to include more people of color?

> How were you socialized to choose the profession that you did? Who were models or mentors for you? If you broke the mold, how did you do that, and what efforts did it take mentally, emotionally, and physically? For instance, did you feel pressured or coerced into your particular profession? Is it traditionally centered on one gender like nursing, teaching, or some other caretaking profession? If you pursued a mostly male-dominated field, how did your childhood and early adult experiences shape that decision?

> Identify the areas in your own life that could be seen as places of privileges by other women. Reflect on whether that place of privilege has been used as a negative lens

with other women. Uncover one way to use your privilege to another woman's advantage and begin to do so with the women in your workplace.

› Choose three major events in history you were alive to experience. How might your experiences been changed if you were of another race, lived in a different country, or were a different gender? Review the discussion above, where Joy and Kami discuss how we can better support one another with this context in mind.

CHAPTER 4

Moving Through and Within

One of the biggest challenges we face as women is the
expectation that we leave all other identities except
our professional selves behind when we enter the workspace. As a professional, showing up as my authentic
self to work would mean freedom from the social dia-
logues that prescribe how these identities intersect
with the workplace and/or isolate one from the workplace. It would mean having supports in place that
allow me to live my healthiest life as a mother, partner,
and professional and a recognition that none of these
operate in isolation. They must all be nurtured for the
authentic self to thrive at work.

— Aditi, South Asian, 38, academic

How are biases established? Imagine you are walking
through a fog. You know there might be something
treacherous nearby, but when fog is present, you can only see
what's right in front of you. You can't see much farther than
where you are, and there are blind spots all around you. The
thicker the fog, the harder it is to see. You know you need to
take it slow, but there's no way to see clearly until the fog lifts.

When we think of bias, we can think of it like a fog — we
don't always know what we don't know. If you aren't aware
of your biases, it's very hard to correct them. We grow up in a
cultural fog that is much like this. We may experience gender
bias before we are even born. The toys and clothes we are given
are based on gender. When we see other cultural practices that

label and categorize people based on race, gender, class, ability, or age, we start to create labels. When we fit neatly — or force ourselves to fit — into these boxes ourselves, we add to the denseness of the fog. We see others enacting the same behaviors, and so the cycle continues and the fog thickens.

We are socially constructed to see groups of people a certain way. This can be due to our upbringing — our beliefs tend to be in sync with the way we were raised — and through our personal network of friends, colleagues, and acquaintances. We pick up additional ideas through media: literature, films, television, and, these days, social media. Social media and online content have become a massive influence on the way groups of people are depicted and stereotyped. Are some stereotypes true? Yes and no. By nature, we categorize our interactions based on similarities and differences. These categories become a checklist of sorts to help us gauge *how* to interact with members of different groups. If our experiences are limited, we only have a few boxes we can check before we determine how to engage, and with limited perspectives, we may interact with gross generalizations that may not be appropriate. If our experiences are more expansive, we have a larger set of boxes to check off before we engage. In the case of stereotypes, the more boxes we have to check off, the more likely our interactions will be less generalized. When thinking through common conceits, such as women are bad at math and men are emotionally incapable, how have we internalized those messages and thought, "Yes, I guess that's true for me," without questioning the validity of the stereotype? In her book *Delusions of Gender: How Our Minds, Society, and Neurosexism Create Difference*, based on the latest research on neuroscience and psychology, Cordelia Fine argues that there isn't a biological difference between male and female brains. Rather, the brain is able to reorganize itself through nerve cells in response to new situations or to changes in the environment.[1]

She argues that when we rely on neurosexist studies that solidify the stereotypes about the male and female brains, it gives us the excuse to throw our hands up and say, "Well, men and women are just hardwired differently." No one stands a chance to change with that kind of thinking. Recall the script analogy from the previous chapter. We might continue to play this script out with no real choice over whether it's accurate about us or not. The power of pervasive stereotypes — positive or negative — is that they still serve to generalize people.

Implicit and Explicit Bias

When Kami took her first job after completing her master's program, she submitted her résumé to an organization that was looking for a bilingual applicant. The pertinent members of the team she would be working for reviewed her information on paper and felt she was a perfect fit. Upon her arrival for the interview, the woman who would be her direct supervisor loved Kami, but the man who served as the director for the Latin America program where she would be working questioned her appearance and considered whether it was professional enough (she had just started loc'ing her hair). He questioned her competence with Spanish and requested an oral exam that he would conduct because he was no longer sure she was a good fit. Her soon-to-be direct supervisor quickly shut down his new requests. This was Kami's first encounter with a true ally. This ally defended Kami by addressing the man's white, heteronormative stereotypes based on her appearance. She risked a professional relationship to call him to task, and Kami was hired. We discuss allyship in more depth in chapter 6.

Many of the studies on implicit bias, such as the Harvard Implicit Association Test and the book *Blindspot: Hidden Biases of Good People* by Mahzarin Banaji and Anthony Greenwald, position implicit bias as the subtle and often invisible ideas and assumptions about a person who belongs to a particular group.[2] This is usually something we don't realize we have or have refused to look at closely. What are our *real* thoughts about a particular group? This could include people of a particular racial group, religion, gender, sexual orientation, class, or situation like homelessness. We never really get rid of our biases, but we can work to identify them and interrupt them before they take action.

Many times, implicit bias creeps up on us via influences that claim a certain group of people are a particular way or perform a particular behavior or value. For instance, consider how an employee's name might influence how we think of them (e.g., Lakeisha vs. Susan). What stereotypes might emerge as to their position in the company? What is the expectation of their behavior and role in the company? Can stereotypes dismiss contributions made by Lakeisha over Susan? What if we throw a Robert into the mix? Subtleties like names are highly suggestive when one hasn't examined their biases.

HOW HISTORY AND GENERATIONAL TRAUMA CAN AMPLIFY BIAS

Theories about the effects of history and trauma across generations are still emerging, but they are interesting ideas to consider. According to a study by Brian P. Chadwick titled

Epigenetics: Current Research and Emerging Trends of epigenetic alterations, our family histories can carry trauma to our offspring[3] Put simply, in 2018, Youssef, Lockwood, Su, Hao, and Rutten found that if a woman suffers from abuse, neglect, or PTSD from a traumatic incident, her DNA can actually change over time based on that experience and that can then have consequences for her children.[4]

How does this relate to bias? Consider how history and generational trauma have seeped into our collective consciousness. Let's use race as an example because it is a deeply ingrained part of who we are whether we acknowledge it or not. Oppressive practices can be deep-seated through generational trauma and one's history of oppression.

When a person experiences a lifetime of racism — from outright and explicit name-calling to being pulled over by a police officer for no reason to more subtle instances of ideas and experiences being dismissed or co-opted by a white colleague at work — these affect a person's sense of well-being and health. Imagine a time when you were felt attacked or belittled based solely on your identity, then imagine that happening at various and sometimes unexpected times on a daily basis for your entire life. There's a great comic strip by Alli Kirkham in *Everyday Feminism* that Joy and Kami use in their workshops, based on a day in the life of a woman of color.[5] In each frame, this woman faces bias all day long from strangers and colleagues. From the woman on the subway hugging her purse closer to her to the men at work interrupting her and taking her ideas and acting as if they were theirs, all day she is confronted by someone's bias based on a myriad of her identities (woman, Latinx, body weight, and class). This constant barrage of bias and stereotyping takes a toll on one's emotional health, which affects their physical health and, apparently as we now know, their biology and their offspring.

LEARNING AND GROWING FROM EXPERIENCE

Clearly, we do not all share the same experiences, but we can certainly learn and educate ourselves about collective experiences that might deeply shape another person's life and opportunities. Knowing that your actions and words impact the people you share space with is crucial for avoiding bias and microaggressions (we'll discuss microaggressions later in this chapter). Many studies and theories (educational,[6] anthropological,[7] sociological,[8] and legal[9]) assert that systemic oppression is a major factor in the continuation of bias, both implicit and explicit.

Systemic oppression is based on the support of institutions and societal practices to segregate and block access to equal opportunities such as health care, education, and political representation. This discrimination is based solely on one's identity and works in a multitude of ways to further enhance our biases. Some of these biases are much more dangerous than others — for example, explaining away a predominantly white or male workforce by claiming a lack of applications from diverse populations, or suggesting that women are not good at science and math so they just don't seek opportunities in those fields. We'll discuss the problems with these arguments in later chapters; in the meantime, we urge you to challenge your biases — perhaps a woman hasn't applied for that data scientist role due to some negative experience in her employment history, or a woman of color tends to be reluctant to speak and stays silent in meetings because she's well aware of the "angry black woman" stereotype.

Microaggressions

Microaggressions are those seemingly innocent remarks, gestures, or actions both verbal and nonverbal that are based solely on someone's marginalized identity (i.e., race, gender, social class, sexual orientation, documentation status, first language, geographic region, etc.). For instance, asking a person of color "Where are you from?" insinuates that they are not from the United States or the ground they are currently standing on. This implies that they are a foreigner in their own land or don't speak the language. It sounds like the person asking the question (and most especially if they are white) is suggesting that *they* belong and the other person does not. That may not be the intention of the question, but we have to be aware of its impact on the other person. You might see someone speaking very slowly to them or commenting on how well they speak English — even though they might very well be a third or fourth generation American. Consider another occasion, in which a woman asks, "Whose baby is that?" to the woman nursing a baby, because the mother and child don't share the same skin color.

A woman colleague might unintentionally assume that another woman is a secretary or not as capable, based on our collective socialization about women, so they might show surprise when a woman displays her expertise on a subject or is the lead on a project. It might be pleasant surprise and genuine adulation, but it's still asserting the stereotype that women aren't leaders. If they are leaders, then they have to strike that balance between being too nice and being pushy, as we discussed in chapter 2.

Microaggressions stem from generalizations about people based on their marginalized social identity. Here are some examples of microaggressions, but most definitely not an exhaustive list:

- Trying to touch a black woman's hair without their permission. (In general, if it's not your hair, then don't touch it.)

- Changing someone's name so it's easier for you to say. (Always ask how to pronounce and what they prefer to be called, never shorten it or change it on your own.)

- Interrupting someone or taking their idea and claiming it as your own.

- Talking over someone in a meeting.

- Condescending to or treating someone like a child.

- Trying to figure out someone's race or ethnicity by asking, "What are you?"

- Saying you are color-blind or you don't see color. This really means you're neglecting to honor that person's experiences as a person of color. Consider, if you're a white woman, if a man said to you, "I don't see you as a white woman." It's a dismissive comment, to say the least.

- Staring at someone's head covering (or just staring in general).

- Interrupting someone's conversation, especially if they didn't invite you in. People from the dominant group do this a lot. It's like claiming that every place and every conversation is yours to participate in. If you come upon a conversation between people of color, two gay folks, or, more specifically, two women of color, and you are part of the dominant group (i.e., white women, straight folks, or men), then wait to be invited to be a part of their conversation — or better yet, be okay with not being invited at all. Wave and move on unless they ask you over.

- Any reference to the "ghetto," "good neighborhood," or "slave labor" — these terms are loaded with systemic oppression.[10] Historically, a ghetto referred to living conditions of Jewish populations and has evolved to people of color living in poor conditions. "Good neighborhood" is a synonym for white and upper class. "Slave labor" is used sometimes to describe unequal conditions in the workplace, but unless you are actually referring to someone being enslaved, don't use this term. It's dismissive of actual experiences of slavery.

- Dismissing someone's traumatic experiences as "not that serious" because you cannot relate to or fathom such trauma in your life.

- Saying anything about someone's appearance, whether it's good or bad. This could be saying they lost weight, are really pretty because they are biracial, a very feminine looking lesbian, commenting on the color of their skin or their hair.

- Being surprised about someone saying they are gay or asking which "role" they take on within the relationship (i.e., the man or the woman).

- Using a person's pronouns incorrectly. Ask them what pronouns they prefer (she/her/hers, he/him/his, or they/them/their). Get in the habit of saying your preferred pronouns because it shows support for nonbinary and trans folks. You can replace "she" or "he" with "they." It's not difficult, and it means the world to them (and not much to you). Don't assume you know someone's gender. Always ask people how they would like to be called or addressed. It shows respect.

- Asking someone what "their group" thinks about something that connects to a collective experience. No one person stands for all "women," "black people," "Asian people," "Latinx," "Native," "gay people," "trans people," or even "American." Everyone's experiences are different and are based on many different factors.

These are just a few examples of microaggressions that could stem from our implicit biases. What are some additional microaggressions that you can add to this list?

White Fragility

Robin DiAngelo, a white academic working in antiracist studies, coined the term "White Fragility" to describe a singular reaction to discussions of race. She explains, "White Fragility is a state in which even a minimum amount of racial stress becomes intolerable, triggering a range of defensive moves. These moves include the outward display of emotions such as anger, fear, and guilt, and behaviors such as argumentation, silence, and leaving the stress-inducing situation. These behaviors, in turn, function to reinstate white racial equilibrium."[11] White people may get defensive, cry, or throw out statements like "I'm not racist," "I didn't participate in slavery," or "I don't see color." It's an important concept for those in the majority culture to understand, as it has a significant effect on populations of color. This type of fragility makes it challenging for people of color to express how they are being treated along racial lines when they are met with defensiveness, dismissiveness, or instant guilty capitulation; in general, they have a hard time standing in the space of their privilege, acknowledging it and claiming responsibility for still benefiting from our continued racist history. White people may not intentionally be using their privilege, but it is inherent and deeply ingrained in our current systems — dating back to slavery, colonialism, internment camps, segregation, and the way immigrants were and are treated. We took a close look at Joy's background in an earlier chapter, where we learned that she can directly trace her access to education from the achievements of her father, and his father before him, and so on. Joy may not have a direct link to slavery, but that doesn't mean she doesn't benefit from white privilege and supremacy. When we acknowledge our generational history of privilege and how that history follows us as individuals and as a society, we start to realize that by using that privilege and ignoring the ramifications of it on others, we are still colluding in racist practices.

DON'T BE A BECKY

In common parlance, a "Becky" is a white woman who uses her white privilege as a weapon or ladder in order to inflict harm on any person of color in ways that may be unintentional, but are definitely microaggressive and sometimes even violent. A Becky might also be known as a "Permit Patty," who has been known to call the police on black people doing everyday things. One woman went so far as to call 9-1-1 on an 8-year-old girl of color selling water outside of her apartment because she wanted to help her mom, who recently lost her job.[12] *The Root* has a great article that defines a Becky more fully, and we highly recommend Catrice M. Jackson's book *The Becky Code*, which discusses how white women may unknowingly perpetuate violence in communities of color.[13] We wanted to address the advent of the Becky here because it's an instructive example that shows white women in particular the harm that calling the police does to communities of color, in addition to the many ways they may be perpetuating racism, consciously or unconsciously. Calling the police on a person of color could end tragically due to police bias, which ripples down to unlawful arrests, which could lead to a criminal record and, even worse, unprovoked physical altercation resulting in bodily injury or death.

When white women undermine and dismiss the experiences of women of color, it cuts those women down and takes away their power. It's important to understand the history of feminism and white feminism in particular, so that we don't take away anyone's right to autonomy or inflict violence on them, but stand in solidarity with them. The first step is to understand those sabotaging behaviors. Do your work, and seek to educate yourself on how you can be a better ally and woman. Some informative sources are *Everyday Feminism*, *The Root*, *Women in the World*, and Rethinking Schools; this last one is great for educators and parents. Usually following a few good people whom you trust will open up other resources. Above all else, stop talking and listen. Be like Kami's supervisor when she challenged the white man in the hiring process. Know from the start the impact of microaggressions and implicit bias on women of color because you have researched, read, *and* listened to the stories of women of color with empathy. Be careful to not insert yourself into a woman of color's life simply because she is a woman of color and you want to "save" her. Sometimes when white women claim to be helping a woman of color they are really helping themselves and propping themselves up.

Here are a few quick tips for handling a situation in which someone tells you that you did something offensive.

Beware of

- Your language and behaviors
- Not being courageous
- Being defensive/offensive

And being/feeling

- Misunderstood
- Belittled or dismissed
- Rejected
- Accused
- Exposed

Instead, stand in your integrity and theirs by seeking to repair and reform your behaviors. Seek to stand up for yourself and others when you see microaggressions happening. We provide you with more specific ideas around solidarity in chapter 6.

The Myth of Intercultural Solidarity

Is it possible for us to feel these microaggressions and implicit bias from members of our own groups? Is it possible for Kami as a black woman to experience microaggressions and implicit bias from other black women? Can Joy as a queer woman experience implicit bias from other members of the queer community? We argue, yes. It makes sense that we want to believe we are safe within our identified groups and communities. This is why when sabotage occurs in these areas, we feel the utmost pain and later distrust in these same spaces. We tend not to address these microaggressions and biases because we want to believe these issues should not exist in those places, so we tell ourselves we are "overreacting" in the situation or have "misunderstood" the person involved.

But we ask that you recall previous chapters. These are learned behaviors. We have been socialized with these thoughts and beliefs, and oftentimes understanding and perception become muddled when we enact these behaviors, because they are based on our socialization.

For example, as a black woman, Kami has been known to roll her eyes and distance herself when she sees another black woman begin to get agitated in a public place. In her head, she's thinking, "Here we go," or "Please don't embarrass us by acting out a stereotype." These thoughts cause Kami to assume that the behaviors of this woman are going to somehow land on her shoulder like a fly unless she makes it obvious that they are not connected in any way. Sounds innocent? It's not. In this case, Kami is being complicit with negative stereotypes, and adjusting her spatial reality and her behaviors to make sure this other black woman is alone in her behaviors.

You may be thinking Kami is just trying not to get involved in what might be a tense situation. Kami might just want to stay out of the way of another person's anger. Perhaps. But let's point out one thing that is a major part of this scenario — Kami doesn't know this woman. Why should she make any assumptions about her in the first place? We can all easily fall into this negative space, and you can see how it can be quite possible for women of color to participate in microaggressions. Because we are of the same identity, be it racially, by gender, or by social class, we take advantage of the presumption that we have inside information and therefore are a better judge. We are justified in thinking what we think because "My aunt is just like her," or "This is that stereotype about us that I hate."

These thoughts are hurting women within our identity groups too, and we don't even realize it.

. . . .

AUTHOR EXCHANGE
On Bias and Microaggressions

Here, Kami and Joy share their experiences regarding microaggressions and biases. They address instances when they have interrupted microaggressions (especially when they were on the receiving end), and how they have challenged their own biases.

Kami

Although I have lived with intersectionality my entire life, I didn't have a name for it until I entered my doctoral program. I have always experienced life first as black, then as woman, and then as middle class, intelligent, educated, and other labels. The first two labels dictated how people responded to the subsequent identities I hold. Being black and woman who grew up in an urban environment, sometimes my middle-class identity is met with surprise. This is a type of microaggression, which assumes that those three combined are a rarity. I really want to address the myth of intercultural solidarity, so I'll discuss an instance when I played into biases.

I have a sorority sister who is known for having a voice that is bit louder than most, a quick temper, and the ability to hold a grudge. She is most comfortable communicating in African American Vernacular English and usually does not see the need to modify or code-switch to mainstream English just because of who may be around to hear. I made it a point to steer clear of her in meetings, went along with conversations about her behaviors with the same knowing glances and eye rolls as everyone else, and found myself making excuses for her when she hurt someone, saying things such as "Once you get to know her, you'll see she's sweet." I say all this because it's necessary to understand what I did, as small as it may have been. My behavior was a microaggression, and it revealed my own implicit biases about other black women who may present themselves in a similar fashion.

One Saturday, this sorority sister came bounding in smiling, laughing, and in an overall good mood. She had just finished her doctoral program and was so happy to be "PhinisheD!" When she came to me, what did I do? Did I congratulate her, celebrate her accomplishments? No, I did not. The first thing I said was "Oh really? What was your dissertation on?" My tone was condescending, judgmental, and not at all what you would expect to greeted with after having completed one of the most mentally strenuous feats of your adulthood. I was out of order. I assumed because of what I knew of her presentation of self, she was incapable of actually completing a reputable program. It was wrong. In the work I've done on myself to be more supportive of women, I had to correct it, and did so accordingly. But what it took to repair that relationship was not worth the sabotage. In that instance, I realized how I judge other women in my affinity groups, groups to which I feel I belong such as African American, scholar, and woman, and sometimes treat them according to that judgment. This is a form of implicit bias. Joy and I choosing to write this book is not just about how white women and women of color can be more supportive across the lines of ethnicity or sexual identity, but how we can be more supportive *within* those lines. It is my hope that this story helps you recall instances in your life where you may have unknowingly sabotaged someone within your ethnic or sexual identity groups. Taking action in these areas is the hardest but the most critical for true solidarity and support.

Joy

As a white woman, I realize I can never completely undo my socialization and biases. I can become more aware of them and work to interrogate them every time they come up. I can also invoke curiosity when my biases come up and examine their origins — for instance, asking myself why I am resisting listening to someone or taking their direction. Is there some kind of preconceived notion or history of discrimination that I have taken on in my thinking? We are not immune even in adulthood. Because I have been doing antiracist work for over twenty years, I am able to adjust my actions a little bit faster. I may read all the books and watch all the movies and documentaries on racism, but society's fog is thick, and it takes vigilant effort to ensure I continue to see through the fog and eviscerate it as much as I can. I believe it's very important to be honest about that because that's where the work lies on undoing bias.

I have had plenty of experience interrupting my biases toward my own identity. As a cisgender woman but also as a closeted queer person, there were many times that my conditioning around lesbians in particular were that they were really masculine and wanted to be men. It was hard for me to imagine how I could be gay or bisexual if I identified with stereotypical feminine ways. The male/female binary was strong in me. I grew up thinking that if you were attracted to women you were a lesbian and if you were attracted to men you were "straight." That was it, black and white. My mind was totally blown when I attended a workshop on the "gender galaxy" in which we explored a whole array of nonbinary identities that don't even fit on a spectrum. When I was a budding queer in the early 1990s in the panhandle of Texas, there wasn't a lot of talk about what it meant to be attracted to both genders. So I remained silent and confused. I always knew I was different in this way and the conditioning I experienced growing up in a conservative

Christian family that didn't recognize the LGBTQI+ identities; dismissing it as "unnatural" further silenced me. However, now in my forties, I find that I am more brave than I have ever been. There's something liberating about getting older and taking the risk of being your true self. Continuing to educate ourselves on the variety of different identities and their subsequent oppressions is imperative when working toward equity. We have to realize that we will never "arrive" at a bias-free state or be persuaded into thinking that we can't possibly insult another person again. We will never truly recognize all the biases we hold, but the important point is that we are continually seeking out the experiences and voices of others to build that empathy and to be a better advocate.

· · · · · · · · · · · · · · · · · · · ·

Action Steps

These action steps are to help you think through those biases that might have been more hidden and, rather than judging yourself about them, examine them with curiosity. We all have biases based on factors like childhood experiences, family, where we grew up, and the media we ingest. Find ways to critique those social references and norms.

> Be curious about your biases in a nonjudgmental way so that you can really find out their origins and reframe the story you tell yourself.

> Think of an important part of your identity (gender, race, ethnicity, ability, sexual orientation, gender expression, language, faith, etc.), then imagine the sociocultural history attached to that identity.

> Think back to a time when you may have experienced any type of microaggression. Reflect on whether you may have perpetuated a microaggression. Take one small step to repair one of those instances. Can you offer an apology to a colleague for a misstep you may have taken?

> How often have you used negative, stereotypical labels (ghetto, ratchet, bitch, cougar, slut, butch) to talk about other women? Identify ways to adjust your language that demonstrate empathy and care to describe women differently.

CHAPTER 5

Self-Care and the Path to Empowerment

> I think if I could be my most authentic self at work
> I would evaluate my actions based on whether I was
> doing the right thing, or whether I was treating people
> right and doing my job well, versus making sure that I
> don't lose the respect of my male coworkers by doing
> things, having reactions, or making decisions that they
> perceive as traditionally female.
>
> — Sarah, white, 32, firefighter

*B*efore we discuss solidarity and liberation, it's necessary to first address empowerment. In order to support each other, our imperative is to heal and empower ourselves — taking care of ourselves before assisting others. We can't truly be in solidarity until we move through the hurt. In thinking about this chapter, we began by inspecting our own practices and beliefs around empowerment — how we practice it ourselves and if we allow space to empower other women. We believe that empowerment is about doing work on our internal "champion" so that we can be a better champion to others. However, empowering ourselves and each other can be difficult in uncertain and often toxic environments.

Defining Empowerment

Put simply, we believe empowerment is the process of becoming stronger and more confident in our ability to represent our interests in all places. Empowerment means standing up for ourselves in our most strategic and bravest of ways. These can be baby steps to empowerment or bold, risky moves or anything in between. Consider the following questions:

- As women, how do we empower ourselves to connect with each other so that we can better stand up when one of us is being taken down?

- How do we utilize moments of incongruity in our own identities, where perhaps our conception of a strong woman isn't evidenced in a particular moment or aspect of our lives, and we want to strengthen our ability to learn and listen?

These questions will be addressed and action steps provided as we work through the chapter and learn how to be vulnerable with our own hurts so that we can start to heal.

In many of our interviews with women, they shared their tendency to bear all the burdens and throw their self-care under the bus to please the crowd. Jill, a single mom, has taken on another project at work because she wants to be seen as a team player and hopes her boss will remember when she's up for that long overdue promotion. She continually feels that she is not doing enough and has to prove herself again and again. She feels like she is just hanging on a ledge with a fragile grasp. She is swamped, exhausted, and can't remember the last time she got her hair cut or just spent time with her friends for a leisurely dinner. Jill's situation is an example of a common self-sabotaging behavior that presents in a number of ways. Her physical, emotional, and mental health is suffering, and she doesn't even have the time to notice because she is in survival mode. She doesn't want to say no at work for fear of rocking the boat. This might happen in our own lives as well. So how do we start to lift the masks that socialization has forced us to wear — those of people-pleasing, feeling like a fraud, or trying to be superwoman? In this chapter, we discuss our practice of self-care — or lack thereof — and how we can move from merely surviving our stressful lives to empowering ourselves to remove the masks and obligations, and walk tall and speak our truth. It won't happen overnight. It's a lifelong desocializing practice that has to be practiced every single day. When we wake up each morning, we must intentionally decide that we will create spaces and moments in our daily lives where we stop and listen to ourselves to honor our inner voices and instincts. When we honor ourselves in this way, we can also honor others.

Disempowerment: The Masks We Wear

What exactly is a mask? To answer this, recall our brief discussion in chapter 3 of the imposter syndrome and the ways in which we do not show up completely as ourselves in certain spaces. The mask is what we put on in order to feel comfortable in those spaces — it's a type of defense mechanism, if you will. There are times when we are in congruence with how we show up in certain spaces and times when we aren't. For instance, at work we may wear a mask of confidence, one that shows, "I got this," and we really believe it. Other days, we feel more like "I'm just going to do all the work so my colleagues have faith in my abilities, but my self-confidence is low." As women, we may go above and beyond to prove our worth and dismantle stereotypes. These masks can be in the form of self-protection or survival; they can be a way we hide our vulnerabilities to avoid playing into stereotypes and they can be a way to protect against retaliation. However, masks can also come in the form of a false ally. Masks can make it so that you claim to have someone's back, but when things shake out, you fall back on self-preservation. For marginalized identities, these types of things happen all the time. Below, we explore different types of masks and how they can affect the way we perceive others, and how we behave toward them.

LIVING WITH THE MASK

"We wear the mask that grins and lies.
It hides our cheeks and shades our eyes..."

These lines from Paul Laurence Dunbar, a famous African American poet from the early twentieth century, speak to Kami's experience with masks as a black woman. For Kami, masks have been so pervasive she finds that she uses them even within her own community. Truth be told, the defense mechanism that has become the mask in the black community, and most pointedly among black women, knows no boundaries. We use them inside and outside our community. It's our shield of protection from harm ... from everyone.

We put on masks to hide our pain from the stings of microaggressions, to protect our hearts from disappointments from so-called allies when our bodies are on the line, and as the switchblade to keep our "competition," other black women in similar positions whom we perceive as a threat to our livelihood and well-being, at bay.

Kami describes her masks as silence and overachievement. She needs to wear them together in order to feel as though she is successfully hiding. But in her position, as the only black tenured faculty within her subject area in a group wholly composed of women, Kami cannot hide. There's a microscope fixed on all of her actions — so she does her best to keep attention away from her. She does as she's told, when she sees a problem she takes a long time to speak on it so she can find the "perfect words," she is overly meticulous about her role and responsibilities so that she doesn't outshine her white female counterparts, while being careful not to allow for any errors or missteps in her work so she can't be called out on them. Most importantly, she shares her pain only in the smallest of safe spaces so that the burdens she carries are not held against her by the very women who cause her stress. As you can imagine, this is an exhausting process, and it's one women of color maintain every day. For Kami, and others, these masks make it difficult, almost impossible, to take part in self-care. While other women may take sick days, or not worry about how they'll be perceived when they make mistakes or if they're a few minutes late to work, Kami has experienced panic attacks over these concerns.

It may seem an exaggerated reaction, but for black women in the workplace, it really is that serious. Many black folk in the workplace are aware of the stereotypes: all black people are lazy, all black people are chronically late, black people only have opportunities via Affirmative Action.

•••

A Common Scenario

Let's take a moment to look at a scenario that plays out in every workplace. We'll consider two versions of the same scenario, one involving a white employee, the other involving an employee of color.

SCENARIO 1

White female employee: I'm really stressed out. I think I need to take a personal day.

Employer: I understand. I hope you feel better.

SCENARIO 2

Black female employee: I've got a lot on my plate and would like to take off a few hours early today so that I can be fully present.

Employer: Hmmm. Okay. But we may need to talk about whether this job may be too much for you to handle if you're as stressed as you claim.

In these scenarios, the white female employee feels comfortable enough to be up-front and matter-of-fact in stating her needs, but the black employee chose her words carefully, and only asked for a few hours off instead of a full day. Even so, she still received pushback from her employer. These seemingly small reactions cause Kami, and many other women of color, to hide their issues at work to avoid having their competence or ability come into question. They would rather detract any and all attention from veering toward those stereotypes at whatever cost to their well-being and mental health instead of facing additional scrutiny and discrimination.

To be fair, these masks — of perfectionism, or the superhero costume worn under plainclothes — can extend to any woman in the workplace or any minority in the workplace. We highlight black women here as most often this is the experience they have in the working world.

• •

MIXED MESSAGES

Joy defines her masks as "staying under the radar" and "never let them see you sweat" (borrowed from an old deodorant commercial). These masks allowed her to slip through unde-tected, especially when she didn't understand school or work concepts or she felt like she was an imposter and at any moment would be found out.

In terms of staying under the radar, all throughout Joy's schooling she had an undiagnosed thyroid condition which made concentrating and learning very difficult.

She was perpetually confused and behind; she was gener-ally in a haze of confusion and poor memory. On top of that, the emotional strain of her parents' separation caused her to feel abandoned and feel like she could only rely on herself. All this combined led her to feel like an imposter — she was essen-tially taking care of herself even though she was never truly comfortable doing so. As a result, whenever Joy finds herself in a vulnerable position, her 10-year-old self resurfaces, along with the same, sinking feeling of "faking it."

For a time, Joy's closeted queerness was another mask. It's allowed her to find a thread of empathy with people of color who have to wear masks on the regular. However, Joy can, if she chooses, hide her queerness and has become a self-proclaimed expert at blending into white, heteronormative spaces. While her ability to relate and empathize helps Joy make connections with people, it's important not to conflate the experiences. Joy can never really know what it's like to walk in the shoes of a woman of color. While empathy can help us relate better to one another, we need to be careful that we're not also conflating empathy with change. We can't let empa-thy manifest into a savior complex or pity, or extend into false ally mode. With all our empathy, the injustice still remains. So we need to trust one another when we share our experiences.

What Does Empowerment Really Look Like?

We've talked about how we disempower ourselves and hide behind masks. How do we get moving toward empowerment?

Let's begin with boundaries. Recall Kami's experience with masks described earlier in the chapter. What if Kami felt comfortable enough in the workplace to say no without fearing it would stain her character or lead others to question her integrity? Just being able to say no would empower black women in their places of work, and they needn't wear a disguise — that of an awkward replication of white women in the workplace. This is critical to our empowerment.

When we discuss empowerment in the context of sabotage and support, those of us with privilege need to understand the masks some of our colleagues are forced to wear, and act in a way so that they feel empowered to be their authentic selves without fearing repercussions, both direct and indirect. We should ask: Can our privileged colleagues place competence and effort from their coworkers of color as expectations, not exceptions? Can our colleagues of color be allowed to grow in their own space, and not according to another's definition of growth? Can we understand that a person's sociocultural experiences are integral to the way they behave? Can we look through our colleagues of color's eyes and be empathetic to their fears and worries, and understand that those fears cannot be easily removed? We need to help our colleagues of color understand that we have got their backs; we'll fight against injustices and for equity with them, not just for ourselves, leaving them to pick up the scraps. As Kami would say, "Are we together in this battle, or nah?" In an interdisciplinary book that crosses the lines of African American studies, media and culture, and psychology, Evans, Burton, and Bell developed a model to support black women taking agency on our collective mental health, aptly named B.R.E.A.T.H.E. The acronym stands for Balance, Reflection, Energy, Association, Transparency, Healing, and Empowerment. Using this model, "one can engage the process of restoration and lifestyle change."[1]

Giving people the space to breathe and be is empowering, especially since some of us are not always able to do so. Women of color want what everyone else has — to be free of the constant figurative molestation and violation of their security and sanity. And giving others this space can be a challenge. We all experience what Joy calls "quicksand" moments, in which we're so overwhelmed — on top of all of life's responsibilities, we have to be allies too? Picture yourself lying face down in quicksand, with the mud and dirt getting into your mouth, eyes, and ears, and meanwhile you're getting pulled down deeper. In these moments, realize that if you stay that way for a second longer, you'll choke on that mud. You have to push yourself up and out, and abandon that feeling of imposter syndrome — the voice telling you that you can't be an ally for any number of reasons, or that you've got your own problems to worry about, so the troubles of others shouldn't affect you too. When you do get up, the expectation is that you'll continue to do the work of self-realization and actualization; you can recover and realign your priorities, and support others as they work toward equity. We can only empower others when we have pulled ourselves up and out of the quicksand.

Our experiences are different across our social identities, but we understand the masks we wear are hurting us and create barriers to practicing even basic levels of self-care. If we can connect across these vulnerabilities, we can create bonds that lay the groundwork for solidarity. This means we have to step away from the masks and the negative self-talk to reach out to our sisters. We have some ideas that will help get things started.

- Empower yourself to stand up when you need to, and also to hold space for connection with others. Consider how doing so lays the groundwork for solidarity.

- Listen to your intuition. When you have a feeling about something deep down in your gut, do you listen to it or ignore it? Practice daily check-ins with your intuition.

- Listen to your feelings. Make a list of the ways you face failure, pain, fear, and other emotions. Work toward the ability to identify what you want and need in any given moment.

- Be the change you wish to see. Give women the benefit of the doubt. Accept that everyone has different boundaries. If you see sabotage in action, be vulnerable enough to call the woman out on her missteps, and then walk her through how to avoid sabotaging the next woman.

- Suspend your need to judge. Learn to actively listen, interrupt bias when you see it happen, and educate as many people as you can. Keep the goal of liberation for all in mind.

··

AUTHOR EXCHANGE
On Empowerment and Self-Care

Here, Kami and Joy discuss self-care, what it means, what it looks like to them, and how it fits in to their goals of empowerment.

Kami

About self-care, there's the answer I give myself, the answer I give the world, and then there's the truth. When it comes to self-care, I can tell others how to do it, know what I need, when I need to do it and how often. I will go so far as to fuss at other women who are not getting enough self-care in a real and intentional way. Alas, my own practice is basically nonexistent. I've mentioned the reasons for this before — I tell myself I can't care for myself lest I be judged by those around me. I have somehow convinced myself that intentional self-care will show me as weak, incompetent, and unworthy in the eyes of the women around me, black and white.

But I try to do what I can. I have many spaces far away from work where I care for self, mentally, physically, and spiritually. I'm also a mother of four, and that position in my life supersedes all the others. So I do my self-care in a piece-meal way, and tell myself I'm being intentional about it just because I somehow managed to fit in that African dance class, or nap on that one Sunday after church, during the kids' nap time, so I could have some time for myself. African dance is a true source of joy and inspiration for me, and one of the ways I combat the stresses of being a black woman in America. So you would think I'd be at a dance class during every free moment I have, or at the very least try to get to one at least once a week? This is the difference between an idea of self-care and actual, meaningful, and intentional self-care.

Intentionality, much like intersectionality, is a buzzword we toss around to sound like we know something important, but we have watered down and convoluted the definition so much that none of us is practicing real intentionality. We are just practicing opportunity and calling it intentionality. But this is unsustainable. When we are working toward breaking through sabotage, we *must* have these moments of rejuvenation, reset, and reflection. Without these, we will crumble under the pressure of the work we are doing. We need to do it alone, and we need to do it together. How can you consider sabotaging your sister when you're having a hot stone massage? But in seriousness, self-care is critical for combating sabotage. When we care for ourselves, we can care for others.

For me, the myth of the superwoman is a big impediment to my engaging in self-care. This myth sometimes has me believing that I must be everything for everyone at the expense of myself. It's the myth that encourages you to do, and keeping doing, until you drop; the myth that says no one has time to get a massage when there's so much work to be done. It's not working out well for me. Lack of self-care immediately puts us as women on the defense. Why? Because we can clearly see our fragility but hope to the heavens that no one else can see it. But we know that they do see our fragility. Then we begin to think we are being judged because of it, which causes us to put our guards up and lash out at the folks we "think" are trying to poke more holes in our armor. We enter into an unnecessary battle with one another as women trying to be the first to strike before we get hit. The problem with this? If we could just relax, we would see that really we are participating in friendly fire. We need a time-out to look at the world with peaceful eyes, and without distrust.

Joy

I like to think I practice self-care, but then I look at my posture, my stress level, my skin, the bags under my eyes, and my genuine fear that if I stop I will lose my edge, my momentum, or that I'm wasting time. I'm always behind my computer or hunched over my phone. I rarely go out with friends for a night on the town and when I do I tend to imbibe too much; I'm like a monkey let out of my cage.

Being a single mom, I cherish the time that I don't have my child so I can get all the "real" work done. I manage my time all day long, but if there is one minute that isn't occupied, I panic. My relaxation time is typically spent binge-watching TV after putting my child to bed; maybe I dig into making a batch of Trader Joe's gluten-free brownies (they're gluten-free, so they're healthy, right?), playing Candy Crush until I run out of lives, worrying about my finances, and finally falling asleep.

Like Kami, I am an expert at telling other people how to care for themselves, and I've even been known to shame a friend for not taking better care of herself. How's that for sisterhood? For so long, I felt like women have been forced to work and live in a system that we didn't create, one that doesn't pay us our worth and has hidden rules that we figure out too little and too late. I also understand that as a white woman living in the twenty-first century in the United States I have more agency than I even realize. I was able to move to a beautiful place in the Pacific Northwest, I try not to check emails on the weekends, and most of the time I draw boundaries with my students, friends, and family. The places where I miss out on self-care is drawing those boundaries in other relationships. Nothing scares me more than being hurt. So whether it's a romantic relationship or in my professional life, I tend to choose the bottom rung position, the safe one. However, more and more after turning 40, I have begun to face these fears and move forward anyway. I speak up when I see something wrong, and I give myself grace when I mess up. I also muster the courage to continually seek ways to change myself in order to change the system. Sometimes I might take a step or two back, that's okay; I eventually muster up the courage and start again. I give myself grace in these moments. I acknowledge that it's normal and okay to deal with self-doubt and to consistently self-reflect. I reflect on my whiteness, queerness, womanness, and Southernness, and continually examine

how the whole story comes together to create the story of
me. I have to deconstruct the ascribed script of not only my
internalized racism, sexism, and homophobia but my exter-
nalized actions and reactions based on those beliefs.

••••••••••••••••••••••

Action Steps

The following action steps give you some space to think
through your own masks. The more we actively self-reflect on
the ways we can be kinder and gentler to ourselves, the easier
it becomes to drop those masks so that others can do the same.

› Revisit the sections about masks, and consider the masks
  you wear. Identify three masks and how they influence
  how you interact with friends, family, colleagues, and
  strangers. What can you do to begin to drop the mask?
  For example, if you wear the "I've got this!" mask, can
  you ask someone for help on a project or task?

› Work to create environments that are welcoming and
  empathetic to all. Be intentional about fully acknowledging the subtle differences between women. To group all
  women in the same category is dangerously inaccurate.

› Think about a time when you stayed under the radar and
  hid aspects of yourself that you were ashamed of or else
  hid for preservation. How can you start to lift that mask
  now? How might you show vulnerability in order to
  allow space for other women to do the same?

› Accept the noes when they come. To question whether
  a no is warranted is dismissive, intrusive, and
  disrespectful.

> Show no favoritism in the types of opportunities available for all women to develop professionally. As an employer, supervisor, or colleague, and most importantly as a benefit to the organization, everyone should be offered equal and equitable opportunities to grow and excel in their respective positions.

> Take the time and the care to fully understand the subtle nuances of the experiences of women of color in your workplace. Notice the difference in the ways people communicate with and about them. Correct any gross generalization and stereotypes in the moment, immediately.

> Assume competence and effort from all women in the workplace. They were hired because their skill set matched the job description *and* they stood out among all the other candidates for the job. Treat them accordingly.

> How do you analyze your judgments of others? How do you create space for an alternative view of that judgment? It's normal to judge, but analyzing the story behind that judgment takes critical practice. Empowerment also means creating space for empowerment to happen for everyone.

> Spend some time considering the boundaries you need to set up to protect your time, energy, and promote self-care. Are you part of any affinity groups or networks from whom you can get the support you need?

CHAPTER 6

Support for Solidarity

> I just want to know what to do. I mean, I know each
> time I open my mouth thinking I'm being an ally, I
> totally get it wrong. I'm not, like, asking to be taught,
> I genuinely just want to be better and I know what I'm
> doing isn't it. How can I get better at showing support
> and not offend in my information gathering and ques-
> tion-asking process?
>
> — Beth, 20, self-identified white Latina, student

When we begin to define how we can show support for someone, the first word that may come to mind is *allyship*. Allyship is an ascribed term (meaning it is best for someone to name you an ally before you name yourself one) that focuses on the ways we use our voice, our power, and our influence to stand in solidarity with women who are marginalized or silenced in our spaces. But what's important to know — and this may be a little hard to swallow — is that ally is a title that is given, not claimed. We want to make sure that we don't just assert ourselves as allies; that's for the other person to determine. Think about this: if a man says, "I'm your ally," but his actions might prove otherwise, then do you want him to continue to tell everyone that he is an ally? It's not enough to label yourself an ally. To truly be an ally involves giving evidence of your work in defense for, in support of, and for the uplifting of the group for which you are claiming allyship. Being an ally is work. At times it can be ugly and/or hurtful, and it can be exhausting. In this chapter, we'll discuss what it really means to embody allyship.

A Look Back

In chapter 4, we discussed microaggressions and often involuntary behaviors steeped in bias. We also discussed how the ways we have been socialized can trigger microaggressive behaviors. If we were to exist in a supportive environment, microaggressive behaviors wouldn't have room to breed and grow. One way to do this is to cultivate spaces for support to reduce incidents of sabotage. By taking preventative measures, we are simultaneously deconstructing and unmasking our biases and socializations. But how do we start? How can we do all of these things and not jeopardize our job, reputation, or work or social relationships?

THE PATH FORWARD

Moving to a place of support begins with our own self-awareness. Let's look at microaggressions in the workplace, where they tend to be common. If given the opportunity to correct your behavior, how might you recast a microaggression that either happened to you or that you perpetuated? A simple way is to practice self-correcting behavior. Recall the experience Joy had in the elevator when her colleague talked about how "huge" Joy used to be, placing her arms out in front of her to show how big Joy's breasts had been. This could have been perceived a number of different ways by Joy, but people who struggle with their weight are usually fine with such comments if they have told people at work that they are trying to lose weight and discuss it openly, or if they are perfectly happy with their body in its current state. This wasn't the case in Joy's situation. She didn't know the woman that well; she had just started working there and had never discussed her weight before. She could tell that the woman started to realize that what she was saying was probably inappropriate and insulting, but she never said anything to Joy. The woman from that incident could have reflected on her words and later approached Joy to say, "I realized I might have insulted you with my comments about your weight. I'm so sorry about that." This is a great way to self-correct your behavior and in general make sure you are more mindful of the impact your words can have on others. Here are a few additional tips for self-correcting behavior:

- Reflecting on your language and behavior
- Pausing and breathing if you think you may be sending a negative or biased message
- Reflecting on why you think a certain thing about someone — what's the history behind that thought?
- Internally reflecting and changing your words and actions
- Checking in with the other person to see their interpretation
- Apologizing and continuing to check in with how you can change the thoughts and actions behind the behavior
- Asking the person how you might move forward in solidarity with them

This may seem overwhelming or "too much" for you. But the truth is that these behaviors are what constructs allies. Are you willing to take these self-reflective actions to correct behaviors in your workplace? Are you willing to help others do the same? This type of support in the workplace can allow the space for women to be more authentic and show up in their fullness without fear of judgment or retaliation.

Authenticity

It is important to reflect on the word "authentic" and its use in the workplace. For us, authentic implies that people are able to show up as their full and complete selves, and not have to hide or mask any part of their personalities for fear of it being used against them. For example, Kami is proud of her African roots. Outside of work hours, she's involved with an African rites of passage group, but although this is a big part of her life, she isn't comfortable sharing it at work. In the workplace, she worries that wearing her African-style head wrap might cause a student to complain, for example, and she could be reprimanded. Further, she fears asking colleagues to review her work prior to submitting for grants or journals as they might say the work is "too black" and not worth trying to publish. This comes from multiple experiences of submitting research to sponsored programs as well as asking for feedback from her colleagues and hearing those exact words: "Your work is too niche. You talk too much about black people. Perhaps if you were more general it can be publishable/funded." In these instances, we can see that Kami is not quite comfortable being her authentic self in the workplace.

We'll spend some time in this section reviewing various forms of authenticity and how acknowledging them can help us move from sabotage to support.

AUTHENTIC MOTHERHOOD

Sometimes talking about their children or the experience of motherhood places working women in a Catch-22. If you have children, you may be passed over for opportunities that your colleagues or boss think would interfere with your family life — even though that should be up to you to decide; while it may seem supportive for a boss to spare you from extra work, you should be the one to make that call. On the other hand, if you're obligated to attend late-night functions or work overtime, it can negatively affect your parenting time. If you don't have children, you might be given more work or have a different set of expectations put upon you because it's assumed you "have the time," and aren't busy with familial obligations like coworkers who have children. When comparing non-mothers to mothers, when the non-mothers are not at work, it can be perceived that they are out on business, but when mothers are not at work, they may be perceived as out taking care of family obligations. These are all part of what a *Harvard Business Review* article termed "the maternal wall," in which women are sidelined and seen as not taking the job seriously enough when they get pregnant or not viable for promotion because they are not as dedicated to the job as non-mothers or other coworkers.[1] According to the Gender Bias Learning Project, 79 percent of mothers are less likely to be hired, and 100 percent are less likely to be promoted and are offered $11,000 less in salary for the same position.[2] This isn't necessarily true for all work environments, especially if the organization is actively trying to change the culture, but for many mothers and non-mothers it's still a barrier.

Men may also lack support by being refused paternity leave or perhaps even judged if they are the primary caretakers for their children. To move to a place of support, we need to change how the actions and policies in the workplace really support a work/life balance. Men can start asking for paternity leave in solidarity with working mothers.

AUTHENTIC LEADERSHIP

What does a leader look like? How does a leader act? If there's a leader in your life that you look up to, or that you worked with, what did that person do to engender a cohesive and supportive work environment? What factors were in place to allow that person to thrive as a leader? In her own life, Joy has found it difficult to answer this question. The best leaders she knows have left their posts due to upheaval — either from the top or the bottom. Many of them have been black women who were sidelined and dismissed. Consider what we've discussed so far. What could Joy have done to support these leaders, even from a subordinate position? She could have openly talked about how well they performed as leaders and how they enhanced the workplace. She could've expressed what she learned from them and rallied support from others. As we say this, we want to also caution that we don't want allies to lose their jobs or jeopardize their security, but the more we practice these behaviors, the more assertive and diplomatic we can be — and the more we can foment changes in the way our leaders lead.

AUTHENTIC COLLABORATION

Truly authentic collaboration means removing the competitive behaviors that tear us down, but still maintaining good-natured competition when working with others. So how do we collaborate with other women in the workplace? If the notion of healthy competition is a bit confusing, let's look at an example of how we can be competitive through affirmations as opposed to being saboteurs. You and another woman are both up for the same job. Both of you are equally qualified, but she gets the job and you do not. How can you support her in her new role? Even though you may be disappointed, you could let your excitement that a qualified person got the job supersede your disappointment. You can have a frank conversation with her about how she might support you through her new role. In this type of collaboration, the person who gets the job should be aware that part of their responsibility involves paving the way for other women to move up in leadership positions. Importantly, the one who does not get the job should understand that it is her job to make sure her colleague feels supported in her new position. Supporting her may look like helping her on new projects and/or recruiting other colleagues whenever possible. Whenever we use the ladder to climb, we need to be sure to put it back so the next woman can use it. If we model that behavior, others are more likely to follow.

If we use the definition of "collaborate" to mean *something created by working jointly with another or others*, we can further define authentic collaboration as almost anything that fosters an environment of support for women in the workplace, including our reactions to women being hired, promoted, and appointed to positions that can continue to tend to the fruitful blossoms of solidarity.

Recruitment and Retention

In this section, we will frame a lot of questions for you to consider. We are not expecting you to immediately address all of these questions, but they are a good roadmap to help you along. To start, look at the recruiting practices in your workplace. If you are able, what can you do to invite more diverse applicants? What can you do to make sure women are applying to upper-level positions and professional development? Are there opportunities for upward mobility, policies for interrupting potential for bias, training and ongoing support for countering bias? Is your organization creating caucus groups and programs specifically aiming at white privilege, but not creating support for people of color by people of color?

In chapter 3, we explored the idea of social constructs. How might these inform the way you see the potential for bias in your workplace? How do you respond when someone says, "There just aren't enough diverse people applying for these positions?" Can you respond in a way that opens up space for reexamining recruitment efforts and workplace climate? There is a reason people are not applying for jobs; find out why. One way is to start with job announcements and recruitment. Examine the way the job is advertised, or the networks it's being sent to, or whether recruiting is being done with a recruiting company that isn't focusing on diverse applicants. Can you or your company use blind reviews by taking out all race references, gender pronouns, and other potentially identifying information that could disclose a person's identity in ways that have nothing to do with the job requirements?

If you have the ability, ask if your company is implementing the following recruiting practices:

- Advertise flexibility in office work hours or working from home. This usually attracts more women, millennials, and people who may be looking for flexibility in order to care for a loved one.

- Examine pre-assessments that allow a wide range of diverse personalities. If your company requires a personality test like the Myers-Briggs, examine what is being asked for in those assessments. Could they hold potential for bias? Personality tests can be limiting and make a person feel boxed in. People react in different ways to different situations and people. Sometimes these personality tests don't account for that.

How might your company craft a vision with diversity in mind? According to a 2018 McKinsey Report, *Delivering Through Diversity*, data gathered from 1,000 companies in twelve countries showed that gender and ethnic diversity increased profitability, and a diverse set of problem solvers often allows for an increase in innovation and business growth.[3] Including a variety of minds increases the pool of ideas, increasing diverse markets and outreach to a wider audience for your product or services. What are other benefits around diversifying your particular workplace?

Accountability Policies and Procedures

What does your organization do in the event of internal conflict? Is there a protocol to help alleviate intergroup tension? Once, Joy ran a workshop in which many of the clients were self-proclaimed introverts, and when faced with a conversation about race, many of them opted to check out of the conversation by stating they were exhausted from so much interaction. In this situation, or a similar one, the facilitators might give participants fifteen minutes to reflect and be by themselves in order to recharge. If they go off and talk to others, then introversion is not the issue, it's that they prefer not to talk about race and are playing the "introvert" card to privilege themselves out of the conversation. When race-based conversations are facilitated skillfully, and the participants can see how they might examine their privileges and marginalizations and find ways to become allies, then real change around racism can occur — but these conversations have to be ongoing and sustainable. We want to emphasize that you may or may not have the ability or access to change some of these situations, but you may know the folks who do and that's a step in the right direction.

Some questions to think about for your organization:

- When examining hierarchy, how might your organization examine their policies and procedures to actively recruit women, people of color, and people of diverse backgrounds and abilities?

- What are the exact policies and procedures around recruiting a diverse pool of people?

- How is your company actively seeking to get people to apply for their positions?

- Does your company prioritize attendance at national, state, and local recruitment fairs in diverse areas to directly seek diversity?

- Are there other ways to check for implicit biases that take someone off the top of the applicant list?

- In what ways are judgments suspended to ensure the applicant's qualifications so they aren't being judged on their identity?

- What does "good fit" look like, exactly? And how might you examine potential for bias?

Professional Development

Professional development (PD) trainings can cover a wide range of topics, including best practices for talking about race, sexual harassment, and microaggressions. Does your company offer PD trainings, and if so, what does the training look like? Do they address race and racism or sexism specifically? When trainings stay more generalized and less specific by looking at universal or shared concerns and not addressing concerns that speak to converging identities, they tend to avoid specific issues that challenge the diversity your organization lacks. You can't just pay someone to do an hour-long presentation. Cultivating the skills to detect bias in policies and procedures is a long-term effort. Individual accountability, small groups, teams, units, and organizations are all responsible for examining their biases in their recruiting and retention practices, as well as their professional development. After implicit bias trainings, what's the follow-up and how is it sustainable? The problem we have seen with these trainings is that folks think, "Well, we had that training, so we're good. We don't need to do more work on it. That box has been checked." This is exactly why these particular types of trainings don't stick. Yes, they open the door, but you have to hire an outside expert to help guide the entire organization so that diversity and inclusion policies are sustainable and are flexible enough to change when the organization gets bigger or otherwise changes. The policies should reflect the evolution of the times, such as implementing gender-neutral bathrooms or ensuring that women are being paid the same as their white male counterparts. We might not have seen those concerns even six or seven years ago. However, now, because times are changing, we want flexible policies to reflect the needs of today's workforce.

The Wage Gap

Women of color are paid drastically less than white women, and white women sometimes use the average of women of color to plead their own case of low wages. However, this can be misleading as it is not an accurate representation of white women's pay. In 2017, the Institute for Women's Policy Research found that while the pay gap has steadily narrowed over time, it is nowhere near being eliminated, and in recent years progress has actually stalled.[4] The gap has narrowed since 1960 largely due to women's progress in education and workforce participation and to men's wages rising at a slower rate. At the rate of change between 1960 and 2015, women are expected to reach pay equity with men in 2059. If change continues at the slower rate seen since 2001, women will not reach pay equity with men until 2152. Allyship is knowing your wage compared not only to white men but to other women.

How Can You Be an Ally?

With these practices in mind, how do you embody allyship and hold space for people to be their true selves? We can't talk about allyship without holding spaces for women to cultivate transformative practices by standing up for ourselves and one another, by interrupting racist and sexist practices regularly. The more we stand in solidarity, the more we can change the systems and institutions to reflect equity across our converging identities. But what does that actually look like? Be careful of conflating empathy with shared experience. When someone shares their struggle, don't try to relate or empathize with your own struggle. Be in the moment with their unique experience with them and for them. Then later ask how you can support them. Awareness of an experience does not mean you are intimate with the experience. You might be intimate with the people involved and you might feel empathy toward their pain, but you don't know what that pain really is. A simple example is the death of a parent. If you haven't lost your mother, but a friend of yours has, you may feel really sorry for your friend, but you can't really relate because it's not your experience. The experiences of marginalized groups in the workforce is similar, even among themselves. A black employee may be able to relate to the experience of an Asian employee, but it's likely that they haven't been treated the same and don't have intimate knowledge of the other's experience.

• •

AUTHOR EXCHANGE
On Allyship

Here, Joy and Kami discuss how to move from simply surviving to thriving in difficult situations, the difference between protecting and empowering, and what each can do to support the other.

Kami

When I think about my own self-care, the term "thrivin' and survivin'" comes to mind. Two words working against one another. They remind me that for many black women the desire to thrive is limited by the need to survive from day to day. When I hear the phrase "thrivin' and survivin'" my mind goes to the theme song of the seventies sitcom *Good Times*. Those exact lyrics are not in the theme song, but I always am reminded that, as a black woman, self-care is a distant fantasy. In many communities, self-care is not seen as a necessary skill set. Learning how to properly care for self so that you can be nurtured, rejuvenated, and in essence protected from the ills of the world can be a foreign concept. We were just taught to deal with it.

Which is why when black women sometimes take "mental

health days" or call for "breaks from the kids" we are met with strange looks not just from non-black women, but from other black women. This is in part due to a trope created as a resistance image to the prevailing stereotypes of Jim Crow: the strong black woman. Chanequa Walker-Barnes suggests that the images of the seductive, beguiling Jezebel, the Mammy, and the loud, rude, overbearing Sapphire were socially sanctioned stereotypes that black women sought to counter with images of a black woman who was self-sufficient, responsible, and dedicated to serving her family and community.[5]

The image has since become "the hegemonic black femininity, as attested by its widespread portrayal in popular culture."[6] The myth of the strong black woman has become much like common American myths like Johnny Appleseed or John Henry, recounted so much we are all convinced it's real. Of course, we know it isn't real. I would even go far as to say that if you infer that black women do not need self-care because we are so resilient, you dismiss our fragile parts, those that deserve care and acknowledgment.

It took a while for me to finally be intentional about self-care, and I'm still lacking in that regard! I am clear about what I need for self-care. I can identify it, and I know the warning signs within myself: disorganization when I am usually Type A, and irritability or illness. These are signs that I need to practice self-care more, but I "forget" to do so in favor of supporting the legend of the strong black woman.

How can Joy support me in my self-care? It could be as simple as a text message: *Hey! Send me an after dance class selfie by next Monday!* If Joy and I were work colleagues, she could acknowledge when I'm feeling overwhelmed and suggest I perhaps take the day off. This encouragement helps, and it is satisfying to stay on track! Even this simple advice will challenge me to find a way to get to that dance class, take my selfie, and send it over by Saturday (if my competitive spirit is high). It would make me feel secure in my need to leave work for self-care, and not worry about judgment or repercussions.

Within your tribe, network, and community, it's important that they know what you need and hold you accountable. This involves vulnerable conversations — and vulnerability is the vehicle we use to get to self-care.

Joy

Although I live in one of the most beautiful places on earth (if I do say so myself) and have access to the ocean and mountains, I'm lucky if I even make it into the back-yard with my laptop. So when I think about self-care, I think about intentionally getting out of my normal loop of working and hustling to simply go on a hike with a friend. Although I taught yoga in a previous life and am consciously mindful of my breath and where I carry tension in my body, I'm not very good about recognizing how prolonged stress has weakened my resilience. We've discussed my back-ground, and how I was thrust into caring for myself; in this vein, my inner little girl, the people-pleaser who wants to be liked and do what's right for everyone while neglect-ing herself, sometimes takes over. Perhaps you can relate to this. For women, the constant pressure to thrive in a system that is determined to keep us down makes it difficult to find more joy and less stress. We're challenged with finding the balance between productivity and maintaining our health, but this can feel like an uphill battle.

When I think of solidarity and self-care, talking to my friends about how we do it and how we can help each other is essential. So how can Kami support me in my self-care? She can remind me of who I am and that what I have to say matters. That our work on this book and in the world is important and needed. For example, while in the process of writing I experienced imposter syndrome. I kept asking myself, "What do you know about empowerment?" and "You don't have a handle on this; other scholars have already addressed it." But Kami said, "Joy, that's the imposter syndrome talking. You already know what to write; stop drawing on other people and just write it."

Knowing that what I do will make a difference in the world is a tremendous form of self-care. By standing up for others, I'm also standing up for myself as a small girl, and for my own child. But in order to do this, my happiness and sanity matter too.

. . . .

Action Steps

These action steps identify ways that we can transform our workplaces by standing in solidarity with one another. When we self-reflect on ways that our individual experiences with socialization have prevented us from authentically showing up in all our roles as women, we can start to lift the masks and create spaces for others to do the same. These action steps lead us into standing up against the maternal wall, help other women thrive as leaders in collaborative ways, and provide appropriate recruitment practices and professional development that actually addresses racist and sexist practices. By naming our experiences we create spaces for others to say, "Yes, I have had that same experience but never knew what to call it or didn't realize other women were experiencing it too. Perhaps now we can do something about it."

> Identify the negative patterns that you've been stuck in as a result of socialization to patriarchy, stereotypes, and

privilege. What is something you can do to break out of these patterns?

> How might we begin to support women around the idea of the maternity wall? Start fighting for equal time off for both maternity and paternity leave. Find the current policy at your workplace, and determine if it needs to be improved. How might you come together with other colleagues who are also affected by these policies?

> Think of one collaborative effort you could undertake with one other person, such as planning a department social or serving on an ad hoc committee (it doesn't have to be with another woman; it could be anyone you work with) and seek to understand their perception of that effort. This could be a personal or professional endeavor. How might you deconstruct your own socialization and the story about what collaboration and leadership means with this person?

> Find out the wage gap in your workplace and seek to equalize inequitable practices by first being aware of them and then taking action within your sphere of influence to change them. Note that it depends on the industry and workplace as to whether you can inquire about salaries or not; many companies have adopted an unspoken rule against salary disclosure. However, at many state universities the salaries of every employee are accessible to the public.

> Examine the recruitment and retention practices discussed in this chapter and see if your workplace includes these ideas. If they don't, how can you form support groups to work on these issues? How can you take power

into your hands with your particular skills and role in the workplace?

› Take an inventory of what you want to address internally around your own insecurities. What triggers your imposter syndrome? What can other women in your workplace, or in your private life, do to help reverse those negative messages?

CHAPTER 7

Support for Transformation and Liberation

> I would feel safe in being vulnerable rather than performing some super version of myself. I think in the vulnerability some magic can happen ... better connections, better ideas, and an opportunity to bring your whole self to work
>
> —Adriana, white, 41, general manager
> of a retail outlet with 250 employees

What might a work environment that is truly free of all bias and prejudice actually look like? Furthermore, what does a space of support look like? Part of this begins with the structure itself—if we look at an organization's top-down structure, as well as from the grassroots, we can see how we might change this structure from both the top and the bottom. In situations like these, it's necessary to strategize from both ends.

We may not always comprehend how our daily actions—the ways in which we interrupt the status quo of racism and sexism—will cause the system of patriarchy to break down. At times it can feel like an uphill battle. If we work together in solidarity, and avoid the seduction of the patriarchy, which often pits us against other women, we can all make it to the top.

Liberation Has Always Been a Possibility

This chapter is a culmination of our efforts — of sorts. We realize the mere existence of this book won't make immediate change, but it is our way of showing others how to open the doors of liberation by disrupting their current beliefs and behaviors so they can learn how to show genuine support and solidarity for one another.

Everything you've read, from start to end, has been intentional. We realize you may already be fully aware of or even educated about the history of the feminist movement in the United States. You may have already taken steps to show empathy for the experiences of the women around you, or perhaps you've been trying to spearhead an affinity group in your workplace. We argue that all of these well-intentioned acts, though commendable, are not enough. Solidarity means integrating the thoughts and behaviors we've explored throughout this book and continuing to practice them. Then we'll see a real shift in solidarity, support, and ultimately our liberation as women.

IN GOOD COMPANY

How do we check ourselves as we deconstruct socialization? Kami, for example, would appreciate it if the other women in her workplace would simply ask, "How are you doing?" This is especially important to her given the violence committed against young black men and women in the United States over the past decade.

Could Kami's colleagues be empathetic to the emotions she may feel whenever another black life is ended? Could they understand her feelings of grief and trauma, give her the space to feel those feelings, and ask the right questions? They might ask whether she feels safe, or if she worries about her children and/or husband being in the wrong place at the wrong time. Though these questions seem invasive, Kami knows that if her colleagues acted on their solidarity, it would help her be more productive. If that sounds odd, when we're able to acknowledge that one's emotional needs are paramount to one's productivity, we can see how extending empathy toward someone, even if we feel awkward or strange about that, may help them in ways we didn't expect.

This isn't to suggest that you walk up to any person of color, or to another woman, and ask "How are you doing?" Rather, the goal here is to help you see how constructing an environment that allows for authenticity can be meaningful to those from marginalized populations. Within this environment, commit to building relationships; know your colleague enough to know what she may be going through. The action step here is to create an environment in which your care and concern are received as genuine because you've expressed it before, and often.

••

Practicing Empathy

In her workshops, Joy sometimes uses an exercise called "Insider/Outsider Perspective." For this activity, she asks participants to draw a timeline of all the times in their lives they have felt like an insider. An insider knows when they feel belonging; when you are an insider, you can tell that others include you and that your ideas are encouraged and welcomed. To get participants to recall these moments, Joy asks them to consider three events, and then do a deep dive into those events: Did they *feel* like an insider? How did they know? How did they react when welcomed by others?

Did these other people behave in a way that made participants understand they were insiders? She asks them to do
the same for outsider, where they felt isolated and were
never or seldom asked to share their ideas, and again asks
them to try to find the center of understanding that made
them know they were an outsider, that they didn't belong.
How did others react to them in that situation?

Try practicing this activity yourself. In the future, should
anyone share with you a story about being an outsider in
a situation that you cannot relate to exactly, you can at
least tap into the feelings that came up for you during the
exercise and extend them some empathy. You'll be able to
understand their experience is valid and worth listening
to. This is another example of doing the work necessary to
become an ally.

• •

Allyship and Liberation

How can true allyship affect the way women bring their
authentic selves to their workplace? As women, sabotage pro-
tects us from bringing our full selves to work, even though we
may see others doing so — something that can breed jealousy
and resentment. We may ask ourselves how another colleague
feels free enough to talk about her life so openly; we may think
another colleague seems younger and more capable, which
makes us feel diminished or unseen. This further speaks to
how we have been socialized to judge and doubt ourselves.

If we hold space for ourselves to acknowledge all our interests and the unique aspects of ourselves, we can do the same for
others of differing identities. Authenticity takes courage — it's
always a risk to reveal ourselves — but by forming affinity
groups at work, and having open and honest conversations

about our individual pain points, we can entice other women to partner with us and do the work with us. These conversations must be strategic and transparent. We have to address the elephants in the room that keep us from doing our jobs well or being valued at work.

Affinity Groups for Support and Empowerment

Many organizations are becoming more receptive to the development of affinity groups, or allowing opportunities for support groups composed of those who may feel underrepresented, marginalized, or at risk within the company. A brief but important note about affinity groups: they are not meant to be venting sessions. They are intended to be spaces for people to feel safe sharing concerns, offering resolutions to these concerns, and creating actionable tasks that can go to the larger organization. In Kami's experience, being a woman of color in academia can be a challenging climb.

There are always looming questions as to whether the fit is a good one, and constant critiques of a research agenda, worthiness for tenure, and an unspoken demand to join every diversity committee on campus — all this in addition to teaching, advising, and mentoring. Given all of this, Kami was pleased when a colleague created an affinity group for women faculty of color. The group met weekly to share wins and worries and offer each other support. Had it been a space for people to complain about how hard they have it, it would not have been a healthy space, certainly not one that allowed the women to rejuvenate, mastermind with like minds and bodies, regroup, and recharge. The women in the group were able to use the meetings to gather strength to go back to their siloed existence as "the only" in their departments with a sense of empowerment to keep going. One of the issues the group saw was the lack of representation on the university promotion and tenure committees. They were intentional about their presence at that table. Why? So the conversations about their work, their service, and their teaching were not laced with bias, stereotype, or unnecessary scrutiny from the committee. If one of the women from this affinity group is at the table as an advocate to speak up for another black woman colleague and advocate for her research, her service, and sometimes her character, then certain biased or stereotyped conversations that might lean toward a denial of promotion will be challenged and in essence, shut down, so our sister can be evaluated fairly.

There are many instances in which affinity groups can be helpful in acknowledging where bias lies and potential pitfalls into which women can unknowingly fall. Without affinity groups, you might not even know the true impact of bias or microaggressions in the workplace. These groups can bring that to light. They can be sources of support and advice. Let the women in your affinity group know what they can do to help you when you are present *and* in your absence. Establish the purpose and some guidelines of the group that everyone can agree to, so it doesn't turn into a venting session. For example, in an affinity group of which Kami was a member, each individual set personal and group goals, the group created space for wins and challenges within the organization, and the group organically allowed one another to hold more space for emotional support, difficult conversations, and action plans as necessary. The group was also clear that whatever was said in the group stayed in the group unless there was a direct request to share certain information with decision makers outside of the affinity group for advocacy. Establish trust so you can stand up and speak out for one another outside that safe space.

Woman Power Up!

Joy's daughter, Ruby, likes to ask if a certain television, book, or real-life woman is using "woman power." In their house, woman power looks like girls and women standing up for themselves when someone says something negative, holding leadership positions, and not relying on boys or men to do things for them. Joy and Ruby also read children's literature about powerful women.

Ruby has a great example that she shares at workshops when Joy has to bring her along. A little boy at her school wrote that he wanted to see girls naked. Ruby found the letter and told the teacher, then told the little boy that he shouldn't talk about little girls' bodies like that. The boy just remained silent, but Ruby had planted the seed. Woman power is also evoked when we see girls on television and in movies showing leadership qualities and not vying for boys' attention but standing in their own power. It's a good question to ask ourselves too. As women out in the world, what does it mean to "woman power up"? What do we do when we're standing alone but still need the support of our "girl posse," and can't alert our tribe when we need help?

Consider the advent of "mansplaining," when a man starts explaining a concept to you, one you may be well-versed in, as though you know nothing about it? Are you comfortable calling this behavior out when confronted with it? A great way to tell men — or anyone, really — that they are mansplaining (or even "whitesplaining") is to ask them to examine whether the person they're talking to is actually asking for an explanation. Ask them to ask themselves if they are assuming ignorance on the part of the other person, or even if they would do the same to a white man, or anyone they deemed to be more credible.

This last question is important, because it's one we can all ask ourselves when we start explaining things. White men are often considered to be authorities in our society, so this type of implicit bias is commonplace.

We have to constantly remind ourselves that we have more power than we think. Some of us may have convinced ourselves that we don't have the voice or position to say, "Can you not say that about that person or me?" Below are a few examples of using woman power and the difficult but necessary conversations to build empowerment and solidarity that lead to liberation — and of course, more woman power.

"MY BEAUTIFUL COLLEAGUE"

Lauren is a leading border policy expert. She was featured on a televised panel discussion; she was the only woman included on the panel, which was moderated by a "well-meaning" (her words) man from Montana. To Lauren's horror, the moderator introduced her as "my beautiful colleague" and proceeded to stumble on about how his wife is still his one and only, and that he wasn't taking away from his marriage by describing Lauren in such a way. It was awkward, and it not only positioned this professional woman, who is established in her career, as a sexualized, codified object that is "beautiful," it also diminished her leadership position at a major conference. The fact that this was televised put Lauren in an even more awkward position. She was already the only woman on the panel; for the moderator to make her introduction about his wife and further promote the notion that women are jealous of each other further instilled him as the rooster pacifying the hens.

Lauren didn't know what to say. She just let it go, for fear of being negatively stereotyped. How might we encourage Lauren to say something to her colleague? How could she have been empowered to speak up in the moment, or even afterward, while being as diplomatic as possible, and without seeming to point the finger at him? She might have said, "I know you meant to compliment me by calling me beautiful, but those types of comments put me in a subservient position that diminishes my role as a leader within an organization. Those types of comments actually hurt my effectiveness with my team. Please just introduce me by my name from now on." That's it. If that doesn't nip the behavior in the bud, and if the behavior has been problematic in the past, she could have made sure to document all the things he has said and start building a case. The goal is not to humiliate him but to arrive at a place of mutual respect and understanding. The more you do it, the easier it gets. Your courage gets amplified fourfold.

We can only breed a culture of respect and accountability if we have enough women standing up and creating a climate where those comments are not tolerated. We have to create and adhere to actual policies and procedures, so that this man, and any other man, would be held accountable for saying such things. Perhaps the perceived risk for standing up is less than you think, and maybe it's worthwhile to investigate more.

DIFFICULT CONVERSATIONS WITH OTHER WOMEN

Tina is a physical therapist who treats people in their homes. She is deeply dedicated and committed to her job. She works overtime, she takes on additional clients when her colleagues cannot, and she constantly engages in further education. She is in charge of her own clients and can easily change her schedule or request time off. However, recently another physical therapist, Joan, was put in charge of managing the schedule only because she wanted to take a break from working with clients. She is not Tina's boss but is in the unusual position of knowing Tina's schedule. Now when Tina wants to change the schedule or take some time off, she has to go through Joan. Joan asks Tina a lot of personal questions that Tina would rather not answer. Joan's persistent questioning and unprofessional behavior make Tina uncomfortable. Tina had recently endured a death in her family and a miscarriage, both emotionally and physically traumatic events, more so because they happened around the same time.

Her main boss knew her situation, but Tina didn't feel comfortable and didn't think it was necessary to share this news with Joan. She felt she already went through the necessary channels to get this time off. According to Tina, Joan is a happy-go-lucky people pleaser, motherly and perhaps a bit nosy. She has also mistakenly thought Tina was 24 when she's actually 38. Joan has insinuated to other colleagues that Tina isn't taking the job seriously and tends to pry information about Tina out of them. When Tina tries to get some time off to attend her uncle's memorial service, and some more time off to recuperate from her miscarriage, Joan wants to know all about why she needs the time off. Tina didn't want to have a long conversation around her private life and, increasingly, Joan's inquiries are stressing her out. When following up with Tina, we later find out that Joan had asked her about her pregnancy (apparently not knowing she had a miscarriage); Tina told her she had a miscarriage, and Joan said, "Well, it's probably a blessing in disguise." A miscarriage is a deeply traumatic event, and Joan's callous response was now layered on top of the power dynamic that kept Tina silent in the first place.

How should Tina communicate her discomfort to Joan? We offer a way for both parties to walk away feeling heard. Tina might use "I" statements when talking to Joan, for example, "I know you want me to feel supported, and I appreciate that about you. However, I feel uncomfortable when you ask me about my private life or why I need time off. Some of these things are very personal to me and I don't want to share them in my workspace." At this point, Tina should ask for Joan's perspective to see how she might be feeling or why she asks these questions. Tina could then end it with: "Moving forward, can we just discuss the schedule without bringing up why I'm taking time off?" This allows Joan the opportunity to share her perspective and for Tina to understand why she might be asking these kinds of questions. Both parties should walk away feeling heard, and with their respective dignities intact. An action plan going forward will also be helpful, so they don't run into other miscommunication.

If we don't talk to each other, then we won't really know what's going on. Admittedly, it is sometimes uncomfortable to address things that are difficult to say, but in the long run you are improving your relationships at work by giving each other the benefit of the doubt. Tina and Joan might even become allies. Tina should be able to work in a stress-free environment and Joan should be allowed to bring in her full personality but with some respectful boundaries. By simply taking responsibility for their feelings and boundaries, this sets the stage for others to do the same. Joan could very well have some things she wants to say to Tina. It takes courage to be vulnerable in these ways.

Repairing and Reconciling

If someone approaches you to tell you of a microaggression on your part, you can still repair the relationship. Think of a time when someone said something insulting to you. For example, about two months after Kami returned from having her second child, she stopped by her white female colleague's office to share good news about a student they both taught. When Kami popped her head into the woman's office, the woman's response was an exasperated sigh and the comment, "Oh God! You're not pregnant *again*, are you?" Might Kami have appreciated it if, even after a few months, that colleague had said to her, "Hey, I wronged you and I'm sorry"? How can we suspend our fear and our egos to allow restorative work to infiltrate our workplaces and our personal lives?

It is never too late to repair a relationship. You can always let the person you offended (or feel that you may have offended) know you are doing the work of examining your socialization around the hurtful or biased thing you said. If you were the recipient of the aggression, how might you talk to the person about how you were affected, how you perceived the microaggression, and how you would like to see their behavior going forward? Develop a plan to check in when these behaviors resurface. Microaggressions will very likely happen, and might be expected as we tend to slip back into old patterns, but these patterns need to be addressed so that they occur less and less.

We can develop trust in relationships by checking in, and allowing folks to keep the sense of solidarity intact. It's an ongoing process; for example, should someone interrupt you or another colleague in a meeting, try tallying the times you or the colleague are interrupted and let the group know what happened. Before a meeting, you could say, "Before we begin, I want to let you all know that I was interrupted this many times in previous meetings." You can also stop the meeting and bring the group's attention back to the person who was interrupted. You can each amplify what the other has said. If you do this enough times with courage, conviction, and persistence, then these behaviors can start changing.

We may struggle sometimes, when the perceived risk of rejection or admonishment is high, but the other woman's discomfort is even higher. We're not perfect, and we recognize that all of us are in this together. Kami and Joy think about all the instances in which they haven't stood in solidarity, and how it's due to a lifetime of socialization that needs to be addressed repeatedly and without interruption. We also have to keep each other accountable for ourselves and for each other. Your courage to address these uncomfortable topics will be your road to liberation.

Finally, we advise you to listen to your body and your intuition. If you question your gut a lot, make it a priority to start listening to yourself and actually follow it.

Say yes when you want to and, most importantly, say no when you need to. When talking with a colleague about a difficult topic, notice your own comfort level when an issue arises. Do you tend to get anxious, nervous, defensive, already exasperated before the conversation even starts? Try to identify where in your body you feel these emotions or triggers.

Next, bring your awareness there and stay with the root of that emotion. Where does that come from? When did you first start to notice your beliefs about that particular topic or issue? What did that look like and what were the messages you gained from those situations? For example, your heart may start to race, or you may find your gaze darts around to not look at the person directly. You may only hear the negative words and not the affirmations. Take note of whether your body temperature rises, you feel tears welling up in your eyes, or you start to fidget. Address those physiological responses. Explore ways to minimize them so that you feel more at ease in difficult conversations. This will give you some idea of why you have a hard time talking about difficult topics like racism, sexism, homophobia, classism, linguistic variations (people with accents different from yours), geographic regional assumptions, belief systems, and so on.

....

AUTHOR EXCHANGE
Embracing Solidarity

How do Kami and Joy work toward living and standing in solidarity with one another and with other women? How do they carve space for agency, advocacy, and growth with one another and with other women? In this section, each of them talks about what their journey to solidarity looks like and how they hold space for one another.

Kami

My tribe is so critical to my development, my empowerment, and my *sanity*. I stand strong when I say this: if you do not have a strong tribe, community, affinity group, board of directors, "kitchen cabinet," whatever you may call it, it's unlikely you will be able to fully show up in support of and solidarity with other women. My tribe doesn't just celebrate the wins with me, they call me on my unsavory behaviors; they see what I can't see. They offer perspectives I never considered. My tribe paints the large, beautiful picture from different vantage points, and that creates the masterpiece of this new perspective for how I see myself within the rest of the world. Without my tribe, I would not have known that I too have sabotaged women. That I too have played into the strong black woman, the Sapphire, and maybe even the Mammy stereotypes as a black woman and judged my sister unfairly through the lenses of these same stereotypes.[1]

A good tribe is not a group of yes-women shouting your praises all the time. We all deserve praise, but it should be balanced—we deserve praise *and* critique. If the people you have around you only offer you glowing praise, consider reevaluating your tribe. My tribe are my mentors—the best advice I can offer is that you surround yourself with a range of folks: people who are where you want to be, people from childhood (who may know you the best), colleagues who are familiar with what you do, and select friends gained through life experiences (not *all* friends; not everyone will serve you). For me, there's an important additional component: people who aren't around as much, but we talk every so often. Within this last group is where my growth lies. Those people—like Joy—may only see bits and pieces of me, but can use those pieces to help me construct my whole self.

Joy

Many of my mentors are the usual suspects: Maya Angelou, who helped me appreciate my womanliness, and Adrienne Rich, who introduced me to feminism and queerness in her powerful poems. In my school days at Ohio State University, my doctoral advisor, Cynthia Dillard, and Rudine Sims Bishop influenced my career trajectory, and they continue to do so. I watched many women in academia struggle to make a place for themselves, refusing to back down or diminish their light.

My tribe is made up of people like the women in my mom group, and my family and close friends who are willing to dig deep into my life, and ask me the hard questions that help me grow and challenge preconceived ideas about what I *think* is possible and what actually *is* possible. They help me get out of my own way. They are great at congratulating me in moments of success, or wallowing with me when times are tough. Deciding to change careers at age 44 and become an entrepreneur was difficult. For a while, I allowed fear to inhibit my ability to live my best, fullest life, and make changes that, though challenging, would be beneficial to me in the long run. My feeling of imposter syndrome still runs rampant like a toddler in a toy shop, but I've got my eye on it and I'm harnessing that little bugger. My tribe allows me to make mistakes and helps me develop empathy by sharing their stories about all of these issues that we face as women. They help keep me open to new ideas and experiences that I wouldn't have had if we hadn't developed that trust and solidarity. I deeply appreciate the women in my life who have sustained friendships when work, kids, distance, and just plain ol' life try to keep us apart. Thank you to my sweet, enduring sisters!

· ·

Action Steps

As we come to the close of this book, we want you to focus on building support and community with the other women in your life, workplace, and the world. These final action steps ask you to reflect on what you have gained from reading this book and also asks critical questions that will allow you to take measurable strides toward support and solidarity with the women in your personal and professional life.

To be clear, the steps you take at the end of this chapter are the *first* steps toward support and solidarity. They will empower you to begin to see what works for you, what fits your values, and what feels most comfortable on your own journey to support and solidarity.

> Take a good look at your workplace and make a list of each of the issues you want to improve. Create a plan for

how you can address them using the insights you have gained from this book. For instance, say you find that you have bias that you weren't aware of before; consider revisiting chapter 4. Use what you've read in that chapter to develop some actionable solutions.

› What are some of the challenges involved in creating an affinity group in your workplace? Is there a way to overcome these challenges or might you need to solicit help? Is there a key stakeholder who can be your advocate? Might you need to find creative ways through lunch dates or coffee chats? Identify who these people may be, but also do a temperature check. Are these the same players who may also be called for diversity and inclusion work? How will the affinity group offer a space for them to get a chance to breathe from that work? How might this serve as a restorative space?

› Review the content on having meaningful conversations and expressing your needs, and allowing others to do the same. What is one workplace relationship that you could address in this way, by using "I" statements and taking responsibility for your actions and feelings, but at the same time speaking your truth in a way that allows the other person to give their perspective. Could this person become an ally?

› Think back to a time when you said something you now regret. With what you've learned, how can you repair that incident now? Reach out to that person. When talking to them, think of the experience as an information-gathering process and come to a viable solution together, so that the other person walks away feeling heard and seen.

The Gift of Support

Your journey has molded you for the greater good, and it was exactly what it needed to be. Don't think that you have lost time. It took each and every situation you have encountered to bring you to the now. And now is right on time.

—Asha Tyson

From the beginning, we have advocated that for women to move from a place of sabotage to one of support, we must look at ourselves, outward to society and other women, and then back to the self. This is a continued journey of self-examination *and* examining our society and our personal and professional environments. We have explained that women can begin to dismantle the patriarchal system by first understanding our feminist cultural history and the key players across racial, class, sexuality, and geographic boundaries. Our personal stories of our own journey toward support and solidarity have provided you with relatable experiences and possibilities we hope will encourage you in difficult moments and remind you that we share this journey with you.

Consider the quote above. Wherever you are on your journey, you are right on time. All your experiences have led you to this book. Sometimes Kami and Joy have encountered women who don't feel prepared to have these conversations. Many times the lack of preparation stemmed from not having all of the information needed to move forward or not being sure how to empathize with other women. We hope that now you feel a firm grasp on how you might educate yourself further, be inspired by other women doing feminist work, and find your own path toward liberation for yourself and the women around you. Our goal was to empower you to be able to confidently stand in solidarity with other women because you know how to access our sociocultural history, you've seen stories that provide a broader picture of the varied experiences of women, and you have points of reflection for yourself and your journey to solidarity.

As we said at the beginning — and we feel it is important to reiterate this as often as possible — this book will not answer all of your questions. This book will not complete your journey to support and solidarity. It has provided you with a strong foundation, it has given you moments to relate to and reflect upon, and it has shifted your ways of knowing when it comes to support and solidarity that extend well beyond the workplace, into your friendships, social circles, and family. However, there's always more to do.

Moving from Sabotage to Support

There was a black woman with a high administrative position at a university. She was respected for her no-nonsense attitude and for her work ethic, and commended for the ways she built up her department to be nationally renowned. But when she was diagnosed with cancer, she kept that news to herself and only a few key people, possibly out of fear of what it might mean for her career. Here's where it gets deeper. While she was in the hospital, her department was scheduled to present to a group in the industry. She had been the primary person responsible and therefore most familiar with the content of the presentation. When it looked like they would have to cancel the presentation, she got up from her hospital bed, put on a wig and a jacket, and presented virtually from a corner in her hospital room.

This breaks our hearts and angers us at the same time. But it is the plight of the black woman in the workplace. Not only do we feel we have to be at our best even at our worst, but there is an expectation that we will. What makes us angry about this is: where were the other key people, most especially the other women, in that department who should have known she was sick and could have stood up for her? Who could have said *no*, we are not going to let you do this. Please take the time to take care of yourself and heal. Sweetie, you have *cancer*. You are literally in your sick bed. We cannot let you do this, and we apologize for making you feel as if you do. Unfortunately, this story does not have a happy ending; this woman succumbed to cancer in the fall of 2017. In our hearts, the lack of support is partly to blame. What would it have looked like for the woman in this story to have received support during her illness? What would you do to show support for someone in this situation?

Had this woman felt support this story might have taken a different turn. The woman above would have felt comfortable disclosing her illness because she would know she had the support of her department while she endured her treatments. Plans would have been put in place to allow her the space to focus on her health and wellness. There may have even been a cancer survivors affinity group on campus that would allow her to safely share her stories with others who have experienced the same. In short, she would have felt as though her workplace was committed completely to her healing and had not allowed her to feel as if her wellness needed to be sacrificed for the sake of her job.

Women faculty in this particular university have in fact learned from this story. An affinity group for faculty women of color now sponsors an annual retreat for women faculty to recharge, rejuvenate, and release with one another through reflective practice and activities that nurture mental and physical health. This retreat has been named in honor of the administrator, not only to remember her but to remind the group of the importance of support in the workplace. This is what it looks like to show support for other women. This is how we stand in solidarity. The effects of this retreat in the years to come will offer women an opportunity to practice support for one another more frequently, so no one feels alone.

There's an important group of people who, for the most part, have been absent from our discussion. We have been and are clear that men must also be included in this work, and in the next section we offer ways in which men can also show support for and stand in solidarity with women.

Men and Liberation

We've been asked many times, "Where can men enter into this conversation?" It may seem backward, but men are also affected by patriarchal structures. Men have their own work to do around the boxes that the patriarchy has strapped them into. They may or may not know or realize how they have been constrained. There may be patterns or behaviors men have been socialized to accept as the norm, not realizing the negative impact they may have on women. For the men we have talked to, there are a variety of ways that their gender identity has surfaced in their lives, from their relationships with their wives and female family members to the way they navigate friendships with other men. After viewing the film *The Mask*

You Live In, a friend of Joy's said he cried during the whole film because they named so much of his experiences growing up, from the need to fix everything to showing aggression and controlling everything, and finally his negative view of women based on his relationship with his mother. In her book *Daring Greatly*, Brené Brown discusses how her work around expressing vulnerability with men found that many of them felt most constrained by the women in their lives.[1] They would say things like, "My wife won't let me express my emotions; she gets uncomfortable when I cry" or "My wife makes fun of me when I can't do something handy."

To paraphrase Brown in both her TED talk "Listening to Shame" and her book *Daring Greatly*, "If you show me a woman who can actually sit with a woman in real vulnerability and fear, I'll show you a woman who's done incredible work. You show me a man who can sit with a woman in deep struggle and vulnerability and not try to fix it, but just hear her and be with her and hold space for it, I'll show you a guy who's done his work and a man who doesn't derive his power from controlling and fixing everything." How can you show up for the men in your life and hold them accountable just as much as the women in your life? Men also need spaces to dismantle the patriarchy, and some of them just don't know how much it actually hurts them too. It's hurting all of us, so why not seek to reach out and transform the system together?

While we're discussing the role of men, it's necessary to address toxic masculinity. Colleen Clemens, associate professor and director of women and gender studies at Kutztown University in Pennsylvania, discusses toxic masculinity as a "narrow and repressive description of manhood, designating manhood as defined by violence, sex, status, and aggression."[2] One of our interviewees, Tim, a community organizer, said the only emotion he felt he was allowed to show was anger and that he had to either fix or constantly be in charge of every situation. He said that some of the worst insults he could remember while growing up were being called weak, a girl, or gay. He also said that's why he felt depressed sometimes. The American Foundation for Suicide Prevention has found that white males account for seven out of ten suicides, and the rate is highest in white middle-aged men.[3]

Interested in getting the men in your life some resources? Some great resources for men are the Men's Project, We Are Man Enough, and the movie *The Mask You Live In*. There are also many TED talks that help white men, and men in general, think through their own socialization. Jason Baldoni, Tony Porter, Jackson Katz, and Paula Stone Williams all discuss the work that men can do to better understand their privilege in the world and what they can do about it. Help the men in your life find an affinity or support group that helps them unpack these issues (if you're a man reading this, consider taking the above suggestion into your own hands). Then allow space for them to do the work; meanwhile, unpack your own expectations of what a man is and what that looks like.

This certainly doesn't pertain to all men; however, there are a variety of constraints that men might experience under the patriarchal system just like women do. Men might feel the need to overcompensate for any insecurities. They might feel that the only emotion they can show is anger, thus any depression, anxiety, sadness, guilt — really, any emotion that's not anger — may manifest itself in their bodies, causing a wide assortment of health issues stemming from the belief that they need to "suck it up" and stay silent. Messages — either overt or more subtle — that suggest men can't show affection or love for one another can only further isolate them. Fatherhood may be seen as a distant, authoritative role, and paternity leave or being a stay-at-home dad can be seen as weak according to patriarchal notions of men's roles. These examples, much like the examples we gave in the book for women, need to be dismantled in order to truly offer support for women to stand in solidarity. How can we support men in their own liberation? Women constrain men in these boxes just as much as other men do. Be careful about what we say to men to confirm their position inside these tiny boxes of what a man should look like or how he should behave. Because these emotions start to build up, alcoholism, drug use, and domestic violence increase. Suicide rates increase. Men don't have spaces to talk about sexual or domestic abuse; they are told to suffer in silence. If they don't have the space or models for forming deep friendships, that isolation leads to a wide range of mental, emotional, and physical illnesses and even suicide.[4]

We all have our roles to play in solidarity and support. We all also have our own work to do to get ourselves to a place where our support is impactful and changes how we as women (and men) see other women in connection to ourselves. Joy and Kami see this journey as a process to experience. The multitude of experiences we all have will be the impetus for change everywhere. How we see ourselves, how we truly see the women we encounter, and the genuine interactions we have based on these views are what will drive the shift to support and solidarity.

Final Thoughts: Self

As you start to unpack the ways you can work in solidarity with yourself and the women around you, the following bulleted list can open up conversations with your fellow sisters so that we can all be liberated and live in those authentic and empowered ways that we dream about. Feel free to add your own goals and conversations and find out ways that you can reach out to other women when it seems like they are having a hard time. If we can all abandon the competition and reach out to one another, only then can the real work of solidarity and transformation change our workplaces and our lives for equity and justice for EVERYONE.

- How do you manage when you are experiencing bias in yourself and about others?

- Take an inventory of what you want to address internally around your insecurities. What triggers your imposter syndrome? What can other women do at your workplace or even in your friendships that will help settle those negative messages?

- Have you experienced your ideas being dismissed? What's your reaction to that, and how might you begin to suspend your reaction and seek the most empowering strategy?

- Gaining knowledge about your rights, what are the policies in place to protect you?

- What helps you create a sense of belonging and value? What does it look like? The more you know about your own sense of self-worth, the more you are able to stand up for yourself.

- Document your experiences with sabotage. You can do a variety of things with this; for example, try to see the number of ways you can express what you have experienced to another person in a way that creates trust, but also protecting yourself at the same time. Remember that sometimes the masks we wear are for our own protection. When do you take them off and when do they need to stay on?

- Whenever you receive feedback, remember that you get to respond and decide what you will take home from the information you've received.

Final Thoughts: Others

Finally, when interfacing with other humans, find ways to extend grace toward yourself and others. When you need self-care take it and when you need some sisterly solidarity ask for it. We all deserve to be heard and seen.

- Do you have an accountability process in place with your fellow women?

- What resources/support networks do you have in place?

- Demonstrate love and grace across gender identities — even to men and the ones who don't quite get it. Show empathy and understanding for the fact that people process differently, and it may take some longer than others to move toward solidarity. At the same time, commit to a self-care practice so that you aren't traumatized every time you extend that grace.

- Acknowledge, appreciate, and promote the magic in our differences.

- Acknowledge, appreciate, and promote the collective wisdom of other women and our elders (indigenous, womanism, and mujerista movements in particular).

We understand these terms are simplified and can be defined in a number of ways, but these are introductory definitions to help you understand concepts that may be new to you or offer a different interpretation of them.

black feminism   Born in the 1960s, black feminism came about in response to the sexism of the civil rights movement and to the racism of the feminist movement. Being black and woman indicated a double bind of rigid limitations that white women would never experience.

Chicana feminism/mujerista   Chicana feminism, much like black feminism, emerged from the need to address the ways in which Mexican American women faced marginalization around race, gender, ethnicity, sexuality, class, and language.

cisgender   A term for people whose gender identity matches the sex they were assigned at birth, such as a woman at birth presenting as a woman. Joy and Kami are both cisgender.

equality   Fairness in status, rights, and opportunities.

equity   The approach to make sure everyone has access to the same opportunities, recognizing that advantages and barriers exist. Equity must begin by acknowledging there is an unequal starting place and seek to correct the imbalance.

feminism   The liberation movement that promotes all women-identified (this means cisgender women, trans women, and anyone who readily identifies as moving through this world as a woman) individuals as equal to men.

gender expression   The myriad ways one can perform gender. It is not a binary of male/female identities; rather, it is an open galaxy in which one can find their own comet, star, or any other body.

hierarchy   A powered-up, top-down approach that encourages competition and power *over* rather than power *with*. This might be based on age, race, gender, status, class, or experiences.

implicit bias   Often shortened to "bias," refers to the attitudes or stereotypes that affect our understanding, actions, and decisions in an unconscious manner.

indigenous   People of native origins who are the original inhabitants of a given region, in contrast to groups that have settled, occupied, or colonized the area more recently (e.g., Native American, Native Pacific Islander, Puerto Ricans and inhabitants of other colonized territories of the United States and Canada, and Andean, Guiana, and Amazonian tribes, among others).

intersectionality   The interconnected nature of race, class, and gender. Intersectionality is about oppression of race, class, and gender, not solely difference. It should not be used as a way to understand differences, but a way to understand oppression because of differences.

microaggressions   Subtle words and behaviors that come from biased thoughts and assumptions about others.

misogyny   The notion of inferiority demonstrated by an assumption that the woman must serve the man just by nature of being a woman.

nonbinary   A person who may have been born with male or female genitalia but now identifies as neither gender identity. Aslo known as "genderqueer."

patriarchy   A male-dominated power structure that gives advantages to men over women and/or other discriminated groups through organized society in ways ranging from individual to institutional, such as health care, education, finance, politics, prison system, corporations, and other constructs.

queer   An umbrella term to describe many different kinds of sexual orientations.

sexism   Systemic prejudice against women as well as using gender stereotypes to discount them.

social identities   Categories of race, ethnicity, gender, gender expression, sexual identity, class, nationality, language, citizenship, documentation status, geographic region, and more. It includes any identity that has been socially constructed.

womanism   Coined by Alice Walker, this term is used to describe the ways in which women of color and marginalized groups are able to celebrate their culture and color in ways they feel feminism has not allowed them to do. It developed originally as a response to the second wave of feminism and has since morphed into a larger movement and field of study.

We wanted to give you a list of women who we believe are not only groundbreaking but who might have been overlooked by mainstream feminism. Throughout the book we mentioned many of these phenomenal women who have contributed to our personal journeys to support and solidarity. We encourage you to read their personal stories, get their writings (some are suggested here), and learn more about their activism. This is just the beginning — there are many other amazing women out there.

Sara Ahmed

> *Differences That Matter: Feminist Theory and Postmodernism* (Cambridge University Press, 1998)
>
> *On Being Included: Racism and Diversity in Institutionalized Life* (Duke University Press, 2012)
>
> *Living a Feminist Life* (Duke University Press, 2017)

LaDonna Brave Bull Allard

> "Turtle Island Storyteller," Wisdom of the Elders, http://www .wisdomoftheelders.org/turtle-island-storyteller-ladonna- brave-bull-allard/

Maya Angelou

> *I Know Why the Caged Bird Sings* (Random House, 1969)
>
> *And Still I Rise* (poetry) (Random House, 1978)
>
> *Now Sheba Sings the Song* (poetry) (Dutton/Dial, 1987)
>
> *Wouldn't Take Nothing for My Journey Now* (Random House, 1993)

Gloria Anzaldúa

> *This Bridge Called My Back: Writings by Radical Women of Color* (co-editor) (Persephone Press, 1981)
>
> *Borderlands/La Frontera: The New Mestiza* (Aunt Lute Books, 1987)

Grace Lee Boggs

The Next American Revolution: Sustainable Activism for the Twenty-First Century (University of California Press, 2011)

Leslie Bow

Betrayal and Other Acts of Subversion: Feminism, Sexual Politics, Asian American Women's Literature (Princeton University Press, 2001)

Partly Colored: Asian Americans and Racial Anomaly in the Segregated South (New York University Press, 2010)

Beth Brant

Mohawk Trail (Firebrand Books, 1985)

Testimony from the Faithful (2003)

Brené Brown

I Thought It Was Just Me (but It Isn't) (Gotham Books, 2007)

Daring Greatly: How the Courage to Be Vulnerable Transforms the Way We Live, Love, Parent, and Lead (Gotham Books, 2012)

Braving the Wilderness: The Quest for True Belonging and the Courage to Stand Alone (Random House, 2017)

Judith Butler

Gender Trouble: Feminism and the Subversion of Identity (Routledge, 1990)

Bodies that Matter: On the Discursive Limits of Sex (Routledge, 1993)

Pema Chödrön

Start Where You Are: A Guide to Compassionate Living (Shambhala, 1994)

When Things Fall Apart: Heart Advice for Difficult Times (Shambhala, 1997)

Patricia Hill Collins

Black Feminist Thought: Knowledge, Consciousness, and the Politics of Empowerment (Routledge, 1990)
Black Sexual Politics: African Americans, Gender, and the New Racism (Routledge, 2004)

Angela Davis

If They Come in the Morning: Voices of Resistance (Third Press, 1971)
Women, Race and Class (Random House, 1981)
Women, Culture and Politics (Vintage Books, 1990)
Freedom Is a Constant Struggle: Ferguson, Palestine, and the Foundations of a Movement (Haymarket, 2016)

Sarah Deer

The Beginning and End of Rape: Confronting Sexual Violence in Native America (University of Minnesota Press, 2015)

Roxanne Dunbar-Ortiz

The Great Sioux Nation: Sitting in Judgment on America (Random House, 1977)
An Indigenous Peoples' History of the United States (Beacon, 2014)

Susan Faludi

Backlash: The Undeclared War Against American Women (Crown, 1991)
Stiffed: The Betrayal of the American Man (William Morrow, 1999)

Sydney Freeland

Hoverboard (film release 2012)
Drunktown's Finest (film release 2014)
Deidra & Laney Rob a Train (film release 2017)

Roxane Gay

"On Stereotypes: Carrying the Burden of Being Strong," *Bitch* 57 (2013)

Bad Feminist (HarperCollins, 2014)
Difficult Women (Grove Press, 2017)

Crystal Echo Hawk

Reclaiming Native Truth: A Project to Dispel America's Myths and Misconceptions, https://www.reclaimingnativetruth .com/

bell hooks

Ain't I a Woman: Black Women and Feminism (South End Press, 1981)
Feminist Theory: From Margin to Center (Routledge, 1984)
Talking Back: Thinking Feminist, Thinking Black (South End Press, 1989)
Feminism Is for Everybody: Passionate Politics (Routledge, 2000)
Writing Beyond Race: Living Theory and Practice (Routledge, 2012)

Dolores Huerta

Dolores (PBS documentary about her life, http://www.pbs.org/ independentlens/films/dolores-huerta/)

Mohja Kahf

"My People Are Rising," *Mizna: Prose, Poetry, and Art Exploring Arab America* (April 2012)
Hagar Poems (University of Arkansas Press, 2016)
"Nine November 2016 in the U.S. of A." (Routledge, 2017)

AnaLouise Keating

Women Reading Women Writing (Temple University Press, 1996)
This Bridge We Call Home: Radical Visions for Transformation (co-editor, Routledge, 2002)
Transformation Now! Toward a Post-Oppositional Politics of Change (University of Illinois Press, 2013)
Transformations: Womanist, Feminist, and Indigenous Studies (series editor, 2017–present)

Maxine Hong Kingston

The Woman Warrior: Memoirs of a Girlhood Among Ghosts (Knopf, 1976)

China Men (Knopf, 1980)

Through the Black Curtain (Friends of the Bancroft Library, 1987)

Winona LaDuke

Last Standing Woman (Voyageur, 1997)

All Our Relations: Native Struggles for Land and Life (Haymarket, 1999)

Recovering the Sacred: the Power of Naming and Claiming (Haymarket, 2005)

The Militarization of Indian Country (Michigan State University Press, 2012)

Audre Lorde

Sister Outsider (Ten Speed Press, 1984)

M.I.A. (Mathangi Arulpragasam)

Maya (N.E.E.T. Recordings, 2010)

Beatrice Medicine

The Native American Woman: A Perspective (Eric/Cress, 1978)

Seeking the Spirit: Plains Indians in Russia (documentary, 1999)

Learning to Be an Anthropologist and Remaining "Native" (University of Illinois Press, 2001)

Janet Mock

Redefining Realness: My Path to Womanhood, Identity, Love & So Much More (Atria, 2014)

Surpassing Certainty: What My Twenties Taught Me (Atria, 2017)

Toni Morrison

The Bluest Eye (Holt, Rinehart & Winston, 1970)

Sula (Knopf, 1973)

Beloved (Knopf, 1987)

Playing in the Dark: Whiteness and the Literary Imagination (Harvard University Press, 1992)

Franchesca Ramsey

Well, That Escalated Quickly: Memoirs and Mistakes of an Accidental Activist (Hachette, 2018)

Decoded (MTV web series)

Adrienne Rich

On Lies, Secrets, and Silence: Selected Prose 1966–1978 (Norton, 1979)

Essential Essays: Culture, Politics, and the Art of Poetry (Norton, 2018)

Josephine St. Pierre Ruffin

Editor and publisher of the *Women's Era* (1890–1897)

Also wrote articles for the black weekly paper *The Courant*

Leslie Marmon Silko

Laguna Woman (Flood Plain Press, 1974)

Ceremony (Viking, 1977)

Storyteller (Arcade, 1981)

Audra Simpson

"Sovereignty, Sympathy, and Indigeneity," in *Ethnographies of U.S. Empire* (Duke University Press, 2018)

"Why White People Love Franz Boas; or, The Grammar of Indigenous Dispossession," in *Indigenous Visions* (Yale University Press, 2018)

Leanne Betasamosake Simpson

As We Have Always Done: Indigenous Freedom Through Radical Resistance (University of Minnesota Press, 2017)

This Accident of Being Lost (House of Anansi Press, 2017)

Sonia Sotomayor

My Beloved World (Knopf, 2013)

Turning Pages: My Life Story (children's book, Philomel Books, 2018)

Mary Church Terrell

"A Plea for the White South by a Colored Woman," *Nineteenth Century*, June 1906

Sojourner Truth

1851 Address to the Ohio Women's Rights Convention (if possible find the original speech, not the one titled "Ain't I a Woman"; the latter is a representation of microaggression as it was rewritten by a white woman who thought it would be better to use a southern vernacular, even though Truth herself never used that style of speech)

Alice Walker

The Color Purple (Harcourt Brace Jovanovich, 1982)

In Search of Our Mothers' Gardens (Harcourt Brace Jovanovich, 1983)

Possessing the Secret of Joy (Harcourt Brace Jovanovich, 1992)

Rebecca Walker

"Becoming the Third Wave," http://www.msmagazine.com/spring2002/BecomingThirdWaveRebeccaWalker.pdf

Ida B. Wells

"The Red Record" (pamphlet, 1895)

Naomi Wolf

The Beauty Myth (William Morrow, 1991)

Give Me Liberty: A Handbook for American Revolutionaries (Simon & Schuster, 2008)

Virginia Woolf

The Voyage Out (Gerald Duckworth and Co., 1915)
Mrs. Dalloway (Hogarth Press, 1925)
A Room of One's Own (Hogarth Press, 1929)

Introduction: The Path to Liberation

1. Catalyst, "Women of Color in the United States," https://www.catalyst.org/knowledge/women-color-united-states-0; *Harvard Business Review*, "Women in the Workplace: A Research Roundup," https://hbr.org/2013/09/women-in-the-workplace-a-research-roundup, Ruchika Tulshyan, "Why Women Are the Worst Kind of Bullies," *Forbes*, April 30, 2012, https://www.forbes.com/sites/worldviews/2012/04/30/why-women-are-the-worst-kind-of-bullies/.
2. We discuss microaggressions in more detail in chapter 4.
3. Shelley Taylor, Laura Cousino Klein, Brian P. Lewis, Tara L. Gruenewald, Regan A. R. Gurung, and John A. Updegraff, "Biobehavioral Responses to Stress in Females: Tend-and-Befriend, Not Fight-or-Flight," *Psychological Review* 107, no. 3 (2000): 411–429.
4. Jessica Bennett, *Feminist Fight Club: An Office Survival Manual for a Sexist Workplace* (New York: Harper Collins, 2016).

Chapter 1: A Brief History of Feminist Movements

1. Coined by Martha Weinman Lear, "The Second Feminist Wave," *New York Times*, March 10, 1968, https://www.nytimes.com/1968/03/10/archives/the-second-feminist-wave.html.
2. Jessie Daniels, "White Women and U.S. Slavery: Then and Now," *Racism Review*, February 4, 2014, http://www.racismreview.com/blog/2014/02/04/white-women-and-slavery/.
3. DoVeanna S. Fulton, "Maria W. Stewart (1803–1879)," in *Slavery in the United States: A Social, Political, and Historical Encyclopedia*, Volume 2, edited by Junius P. Rodriguez (Santa Barbara, CA: ABC-CLIO, 2007), p. 463.
4. Marilyn Richardson, "Maria W. Stewart," in *Oxford Companion to African American Literature*, edited by William L.

Andrews, Frances Smith Foster, and Trudier Harris (New York: Oxford University Press, 1997), 379–380.

5. Patricia Hill Collins, *Black Feminist Thought: Knowledge, Consciousness and the Politics of Empowerment* (New York: Routledge, 2009).

6. Mark Leibovich, "Rights vs. Rights: An Improbable Collision Course," *New York Times*, January 13, 2008, https://www.nytimes.com/2008/01/13/weekinreview/13leibovich.html; Michele Bollinger and Tran Dao X, eds., *101 Changemakers: Rebels and Radicals Who Changed US History* (Chicago: Haymarket, 2012).

7. John Woolley and Gerhard Peters, American Presidency Project, https://www.presidency.ucsb.edu/.

8. Thomas Volscho, "Sterilization and Women of Color," *Racism Review*, September 22, 2007, http://www.racismreview.com/blog/2007/09/22/sterilization-and-women-of-color/.

9. Lisa Ko, "Unwanted Sterilization and Eugenics Programs in the United States," *Independent Lens*, January 29, 2016, http://www.pbs.org/independentlens/blog/unwanted-sterilization-and-eugenics-programs-in-the-united-states/.

10. National Asian Pacific American Women's Forum, https://www.napawf.org/reproductivejustice.html.

11. Alice Walker, "Coming Apart," in *You Can't Keep a Good Woman Down* (San Diego: Harcourt, 2004).

12. Patricia Hill Collins, *Black Feminist Thought* (New York: Routledge, 2000).

13. Alvin M. Josephy, Joane Nagel, and Troy R. Johnson, eds., *Red Power: The American Indians' Fight for Freedom*, 2nd ed. (Lincoln: University of Nebraska Press), pp. 51–52.

14. "Radiation: 'Dangerous to Pine Ridge Women' W.A.R.N. Study Says," *Akwesasne News*, early spring 1980, http://www.oocities.org/lakotastudentalliance/warnstudy_radiation.pdf.

15. Becky Thompson, "Multiracial Feminism: Recasting the Chronology of Second Wave Feminism," *Feminist Studies* 28, no. 2, Second Wave Feminism in the United States (Summer 2002): 336–360.

16. Yoonj Kim, "#NotYourAsianSidekick Is a Civil Rights Movement for Asian American Women," December 17, 2013, *Guardian*, https://www.theguardian.com/commentisfree/2013/dec/17/not-your-asian-sidekick-asian-women-feminism.

17. Shruti Mukkamala and Karen L. Suyemoto, "Racialized Sexism/Sexualized Racism: A Multimethod Study of Intersectional Experiences of Discrimination for Asian American Women," *Asian American Journal of Psychology* 9, no. 1 (2018): 32–46.

18. Susan Muaddi Darraj, "Understanding the Other Sister: The Case of Arab Feminism," *Monthly Review*, March 2002, https://monthlyreview.org/2002/03/01/understanding-the-other-sister-the-case-of-arab-feminism/.

19. Noor Almohsin, "10 Arab American Female Activists," *Arab America*, March 21, 2018, https://www.arabamerica.com/arab-female-activists/.

20. Emi Koyama, "The Transfeminist Manifesto," in *Catching a Wave: Reclaiming Feminism for the Twenty-First Century*, edited by Rory Dicker and Alison Piepmeier (Lebanon, NH: Northeastern University Press, 2003), http://eminism.org/readings/pdf-rdg/tfmanifesto.pdf.

21. Kimberlé Crenshaw, "Demarginalizing the Intersection of Race and Sex: A Black Feminist Critique of Antidiscrimination Doctrine," University of Chicago Legal Forum, 1989, http://chicagounbound.uchicago.edu/uclf/vol1989/iss1/8.

22. Crenshaw, "Mapping the Margins: Intersectionality, Identity Politics, and Violence Against Women of Color," in *The Public Nature of Private Violence*, edited by Martha Albertson Fineman and Roxanne Mykitiuk (New York: Routledge, 1994), pp. 93–118.

23. Wisdom of the Elders, "Turtle Island Storyteller LaDonna Brave Bull Allard," http://www.wisdomoftheelders.org/turtle-island-storyteller-ladonna-brave-bull-allard/.

24. Noor Almohsin, "10 Arab American Female Activists," *Arab America*, March 21, 2018, https://www.arabamerica.com/arab-female-activists/.

25. Coined in Susan Cox and Lee Galda, "Multicultural Literature: Mirrors and Windows on a Global Community," *Reading
Teacher* 43, no. 8 (1990): 582–589.

Chapter 2: The Pervasive Patriarchy

1. Terrance Real, *How Can I Get Through to You? Closing the Intimacy Gap Between Men and Women* (New York: Scribner, 2003).
Also see https://findingbrave.org/episode-4-gender-power-
relationships-crushing-effects-patriarchy-terry-real/.

2. bell hooks, *Feminism Is for Everybody: Passionate Politics* (Boston: South End Press, 2000); "Understanding Patriarchy,"
http://imaginenoborders.org/pdf/zines/
UnderstandingPatriarchy.pdf.

3. See, for example, Peter L. Berger and Thomas Luckmann, *The
Social Construction of Reality* (New York: Anchor Books, 1966).

4. Ban Bossy, http://banbossy.com/.

5. Catalyst, "Catalyst Study Exposes How Gender-Based Stereotyping Sabotages Women in the Workplace," https://www
.catalyst.org/media/catalyst-study-exposes-how-gender-
based-stereotyping-sabotages-women-workplace.

6. Kim Elsesser, *Sex and the Office* (Lanham, MD: Taylor Trade,
2015).

7. W. E. B. Du Bois, *The Souls of Black Folk* (Mineola, NY: Dover,
1994 [1903]), p. 2.

Chapter 3: The Power of Privilege

1. Michigan Civil Rights Commission, *The Flint Water Crisis:
Systemic Racism Through the Lens of Flint*, February 17, 2017,
https://www.michigan.gov/documents/mdcr/
VFlintCrisisRep-F-Edited3-13-17_554317_7.pdf.

2. John Rosales, "Challenging Institutional Racism in Education," National Education Association, https://ra.nea
.org/2016/07/02/challenging-institutional-racism-education/.

3. Django Paris, "Culturally Sustaining Pedagogy: A Needed
Change in Stance, Terminology, and Practice," *Educational
Researcher* 41, no. 3 (2012): 93–97.

4. G. Ladson-Billings, "Toward a Theory of Culturally Relevant Pedagogy," *American Educational Research Journal* 32, no. 3 (1995): 465–491; Lisa Delpit, *Other People's Children: Cultural Conflict in the Classroom* (New York: New Press, 1995).

5. Paris, "Culturally Sustaining Pedagogy," 93.

Chapter 4: Moving Through and Within

1. Cordelia Fine, *Delusions of Gender: How Our Minds, Society, and Neurosexism Create Difference* (New York: Norton, 2010).

2. Mahzarin Banaji and Anthony Greenwald, *Blindspot: Hidden Biases of Good People* (New York: Delacorte, 2013).

3. Brian P. Chadwick, ed., *Epigenetics: Current Research and Emerging Trends* (Poole, UK: Caister Academic Press, 2015).

4. Nagy A. Youssef, Laura Lockwood, Shaoyong Su, Guang Hao, and Bart P. F. Rutten, "The Effects of Trauma, with or without PTSD, on the Transgenerational DNA Methylation Alterations in Human Offsprings," *Brain Sciences* 8, no. 5 (2018): 83.

5. Alli Kirkham, "This Is the Perfect Illustration of Why Microaggressions Hurt," *Everyday Feminism*, October 5, 2015, https://everydayfeminism.com/2015/10/why-microaggressions-hurt/.

6. Paulo Freire, *Pedagogy of the Oppressed* (New York: Continuum, 1970).

7. B. Levinson, D. Foley, and D. C. Holland, *The Cultural Production of the Educated Person: Critical Ethnographies of Schooling and Local Practice* (Albany: State University of New York Press, 1996).

8. Cornel West, *Race Matters*, 25th anniversary ed. (Boston: Beacon, 2017).

9. Michelle Alexander, *The New Jim Crow: Mass Incarceration in the Age of Colorblindness* (New York: New Press, 2012).

10. Zoë Triska, "These Words You Use Every Day Have Racist/Prejudiced Pasts, and You Had No Idea," *Huffington Post*, October 25, 2013, https://www.huffingtonpost.com/2013/10/24/offensive-words-_n_4144472.html.

11. Robin DiAngelo, "White Fragility," *International Journal of Critical Pedagogy* 3, no. 3 (2011): 54–70, at 54.

12. Niraj Chokshi, "White Woman Nicknamed 'Permit Patty' Regrets Confrontation with Black Girl Selling Water," *New York Times*, June 25, 2018, https://www.nytimes.com/2018/06/25/us/permit-patty-black-girl-water.html.

13. Michael Harriot, "The 5 Types of Becky," *The Root*, https://www.theroot.com/the-five-types-of-becky-1798543210; Catrice M. Jackson, *The Becky Code*, http://www.thebeckycode.com/.

Chapter 5: Self-Care and the Path to Empowerment

1. S. Y. Evans, K. Bell, and N. K. Burton, *Black Women's Mental Health: Balancing Strength and Vulnerability* (Albany: State University of New York Press, 2017).

Chapter 6: Support for Solidarity

1. Joan C. Williams, "The Maternal Wall," *Harvard Business Review*, October 2004, https://hbr.org/2004/10/the-maternal-wall.

2. Gender Bias Learning Project, "Maternal Wall," https://genderbiasbingo.com/maternal-wall/.

3. Vivian Hunt, Lareina Yee, Sara Prince, and Sundiatu Dixon-Fyle, "Delivering through Diversity," McKinsey and Company, 2018, https://www.mckinsey.com/business-functions/organization/our-insights/delivering-through-diversity.

4. Ariane Hegewisch and Emma Williams-Baron, "The Gender Wage Gap: 2017 Earnings Differences by Race and Ethnicity," March 7, 2018, Institute for Women's Policy Research, https://iwpr.org/publications/gender-wage-gap-2017-race-ethnicity/

5. Carolyn M. West, "Mammy, Sapphire, and Jezebel: Historical Images of Black Women and Their Implications for Psychotherapy," *Psychotherapy: Theory, Research, Practice, Training* 32, no. 3 (1995): 458–466.

6. Chanequa Walker-Barnes, "When the Bough Breaks: The Strong Black Woman and the Embodiment of Stress," in *Black Women's Mental Health*, edited by Evans, Bell, and Burton.

Chapter 7: Support for Transformation and Liberation

1. Carolyn M. West, "Images of Black Women," in *Women's Studies Encyclopedia*, ed. Helen Tierney (Westport, CT: Greenwood, 1999), pp. 680–681; West, "Mammy, Sapphire, and Jezebel: Historical Images of Black Women and Their Implications for Psychotherapy," *Psychotherapy: Theory, Research, Practice, Training* 32, no. 3 (1995): 458–466.

Conclusion: The Gift of Support

1. Brené Brown, *Daring Greatly: How the Courage to Be Vulnerable Transforms the Way We Live, Love, Parent, and Lead* (New York: Gotham Books, 2012); see also https://www.ted.com/talks/ brene_brown_listening_to_shame.

2. Colleen Clemens, "What We Mean When We Say, 'Toxic Masculinity,'" *Teaching Tolerance*, December 11, 2017, https://www .tolerance.org/magazine/what-we-mean-when-we-say-toxic-masculinity.

3. American Foundation for Suicide Prevention, https://afsp .org/about-suicide/suicide-statistics/.

4. National Institute of Mental Health, https://www.nimh.nih .gov/health/statistics/suicide.shtml.

First we would like to thank Tiffany Jana. Without your initial introduction to our new publishing family, this work would still be a fabulous idea and coffee chat between two colleagues.

We would then like to thank Anna Leinberger of Berrett-Koehler Publishing, for your dedication to our project. You believed in our work from the very beginning, and we are so grateful for all the ways you guided us, supported us, and nudged us to meet deadlines, all of which contributed to this wonderful project. We are eternally grateful for your commitment to us and this work. We would also like to thank the entire Berrett-Koehler team for all of the hard work you each put into the design, marketing, and promoting of this important and timely issue.

Thank you to our development editor, Nana Twumasi, for your guidance through our manuscript. Your insight has given us a project we are most proud of—one that tells a story with the greatest impact not only for our readers but for us as authors. Thank you also to each person who reviewed and provided endorsements for our work. Your feedback and encouraging words further show the need for this work in our current society and give us a glimpse into the types of discussions that will bloom because of it.

We also acknowledge each and every woman who shared their stories, joyful, painful, and helpful, in order to make this project rich with your voices. Thank you so much! We hope that we honored your hearts and your voices in ways that will benefit each and every reader of this book.

It is never easy to be a scholar mom, for the mom or the family. Thank you to our families for your support during our late night writing sessions, our conference calls during family time, and most of all your patience through all of it. Of course we love you, but we appreciate the ways in which this project is very much a labor of love from you all as well: Ruby, Jasira, Jason, Jachin, Jeffrey, and Jeff, without your enduring love and support, we would not have been able to get this into our readers' hands.

Page references followed by *fig* indicate an illustrated figure.

Index

Index

Joy L. Wiggins, Ph.D., received her doctorate from Ohio State University in multicultural and social justice education. She is the founder and CEO of Joy Wiggins, Ph.D.: Equity and Inclusion Consulting, which provides speaking, facilitation, and mentorship opportunities on the topics of power, privilege, racial and gender justice, and liberation. She teaches multicultural children's literature, literacy, and English language learning in the elementary education department at Western Washington University in Bellingham, Washington. She has published extensively in international and national scholarly journals and for community network publications.

Dr. Wiggins has spent the last fifteen years working on understanding our cultural identities and perceptions of how we navigate the world. Her current work focuses on actively evaluating the way we are socially constructed and how that plays into our daily intercultural communicative experiences. Her goal is to facilitate transformative learning opportunities infused with empathy, compassion, and perspective taking. Much of Dr. Wiggins's work and teaching has been in teacher education as a professor and K–12 education. Dr. Wiggins holds a bachelor's degree from Texas Tech University in multidisciplinary studies and English, a master's degree in literacy education from Western Washington University, and a doctorate in multicultural and social justice in education.

**Kami J. Anderson,** Ph.D., has published extensively in both English and Spanish in scholarly and trade journals as well as in national U.S. news publications. She has traveled to seventeen countries around the globe for academic and professional endeavors. She is a strong advocate for study abroad, in particular for students of color. A loving mother to four wonderful, bilingual children, Kami has a vested interest in the construction of identity with bilingualism. Her book *Language, Identity, and Choice: Raising Bilingual Children in a Global Society* (Lanham, MD: Lexington Books, 2015) talks about her own experiences raising her children.

Dr. Anderson has spent the past two decades immersed in languages and cultures and intercultural training and evaluation. From working overseas in relief and development to teaching language in the classroom, to molding future intercultural scholars in the lecture hall, Dr. Anderson has always kept a tight grip on her passion and compassion for others and differences in language acquisition. Her primary focus is family empowerment through language acquisition with an emphasis on application and confidence. She holds a bachelor's degree in Spanish from Spelman College, a master's degree in international affairs/interdisciplinary studies in international communication and anthropology from American University, and a Ph.D. in communication and culture from Howard University.

Berrett–Koehler
Publishers

Berrett-Koehler is an independent publisher dedicated to an ambitious mission: *Connecting people and ideas to create a world that works for all.*

Our publications span many formats, including print, digital, audio, and video. We also offer online resources, training, and gatherings. And we will continue expanding our products and services to advance our mission.

We believe that the solutions to the world's problems will come from all of us, working at all levels: in our society, in our organizations, and in our own lives. Our publications and resources offer pathways to creating a more just, equitable, and sustainable society. They help people make their organizations more humane, democratic, diverse, and effective (and we don't think there's any contradiction there). And they guide people in creating positive change in their own lives and aligning their personal practices with their aspirations for a better world.

And we strive to practice what we preach through what we call "The BK Way." At the core of this approach is *stewardship,* a deep sense of responsibility to administer the company for the benefit of all of our stakeholder groups, including authors, customers, employees, investors, service providers, sales partners, and the communities and environment around us. Everything we do is built around stewardship and our other core values of *quality, partnership, inclusion,* and *sustainability.*

This is why Berrett-Koehler is the first book publishing company to be both a B Corporation (a rigorous certification) and a benefit corporation (a for-profit legal status), which together require us to adhere to the highest standards for corporate, social, and environmental performance. And it is why we have instituted many pioneering practices (which you can learn about at www.bkconnection.com), including the Berrett-Koehler Constitution, the Bill of Rights and Responsibilities for BK Authors, and our unique Author Days.

We are grateful to our readers, authors, and other friends who are supporting our mission. We ask you to share with us examples of how BK publications and resources are making a difference in your lives, organizations, and communities at www.bkconnection.com/impact.

Dear reader,

Thank you for picking up this book and welcome to the worldwide BK community! You're joining a special group of people who have come together to create positive change in their lives, organizations, and communities.

What's BK all about?

Our mission is to connect people and ideas to create a world that works for all.

Why? Our communities, organizations, and lives get bogged down by old paradigms of self-interest, exclusion, hierarchy, and privilege. But we believe that can change. That's why we seek the leading experts on these challenges—and share their actionable ideas with you.

A welcome gift

To help you get started, we'd like to offer you a **free copy** of one of our bestselling ebooks:

www.bkconnection.com/welcome

When you claim your **free ebook**, you'll also be subscribed to our blog.

Our freshest insights

Access the best new tools and ideas for leaders at all levels on our blog at ideas.bkconnection.com.

Sincerely,

Your friends at Berrett-Koehler

MIX
Paper from
responsible sources
FSC® C002589